The *Embroidery* Book

Christen Brown

Visual Resource of Color & Design

149 Stitches • Step-by-Step Guide

C&T PUBLISHING

Text copyright © 2016 by Christen Brown

Photography and artwork copyright © 2016 by C&T Publishing, Inc.

Publisher: Amy Marson

Creative Director: Gailen Runge

Editor: Liz Aneloski

Technical Editor: Helen Frost

Cover/Book Designer: April Mostek

Production Coordinator: Zinnia Heinzmann

Production Editor: Jennifer Warren

Illustrator: Mary E. Flynn

Photo Assistant: Carly Jean Marin

Quilt and instructional photography by Diane Pedersen, unless otherwise noted

Published by C&T Publishing, Inc., P.O. Box 1456, Lafayette, CA 94549

Library of Congress Cataloging-in-Publication Data

Names: Brown, Christen (Christen Joan) author.

Title: The embroidery book : visual resource of color & design - 149 stitches - step-by-step guide / Christen Brown.

Description: Lafayette, CA : C&T Publishing, [2016]

Identifiers: LCCN 2016016918 | ISBN 9781617452246 (softcover)

Subjects: LCSH: Embroidery.

Classification: LCC TT770 .B8877 2016 | DDC 746.44--dc23

LC record available at https://lccn.loc.gov/2016016918

Printed in China

10 9 8 7 6 5 4 3 2 1

HAPPY CREATING

I dedicate this book to all my students, both past and present. Thank you for giving me this opportunity to share my knowledge with you. May you always find the time to enjoy the creative adventure.

With Love, Christen

Flutterbye

Blue Heart Etui

MY BIGGEST FANS

To my husband, Kevin, and daughter, Gwen—thank you for your unconditional love and support and for allowing me to play in my room.

Love you both!

SPECIAL ACKNOWLEDGMENTS

I have been fortunate to have the most wonderful people helping me throughout the process of designing, writing, editing, and photographing for this book. I would like to thank each and every person whose expertise has touched these pages. Special thanks go to Liz, my editor—you know how special you are, and I do appreciate you.

Thank you also to those who have bequeathed their precious bits of lace, fabric, trims, and buttons to me. I have enjoyed giving them a permanent home in my creations.

Ribbon-embroidered brooches

CONTENTS

VISUAL GUIDE

Blanket and Buttonhole Stitches

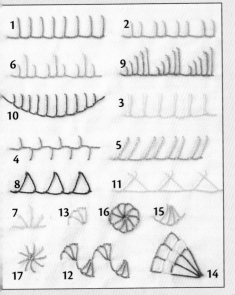

1. Blanket Stitch (page 116)

2. Blanket Stitch Grouped Even (page 116)

3. Blanket Stitch Up and Down (page 116)

4. Blanket Stitch Zipper Row (page 116)

5. Blanket Stitch Angled (page 116)

6. Blanket Stitch Short-Long-Short (page 116)

7. Blanket Stitch Stalk (page 117)

8. Blanket Stitch Closed (page 117)

9. Musical Notes Stitch (page 117)

10. Blanket Stitch Dipped (page 117)

11. Blanket Stitch Crossed (page 117)

12. Shell Stitch Row (page 117)

13. Shell Stitch (page 118)

14. Blanket Stitch Cobweb (page 118)

15. Bell Flower Stitch (page 118)

16. Buttonhole Circle Stitch (page 118)

17. Blanket Stitch Flower (page 118)

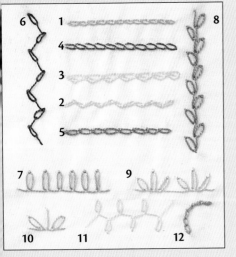

Chain and Looped Stitches

1. Chain Stitch (page 120)

2. Chain Stitch Zigzag (page 120)

3. Chain Stitch Double (page 120)

4. Chain Stitch Open (page 120)

5. Chain Stitch Cable (page 120)

6. Chain Stitch Feathered (page 120)

7. Looped Blanket Stitch (page 121)

8. Looped Feather Stitch (page 121)

9. Loop Stitch Petal Row (page 121)

10. Loop Stitch Leaves and Stalk (page 121)

11. Looped Cretan Stitch (page 121)

12. Chain Stitch Loop (page 121)

Chevron, Cretan, Cross, and Herringbone Stitches

Feather Stitches

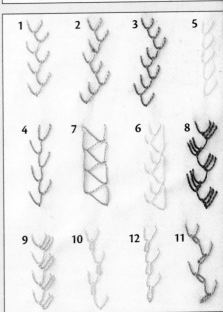

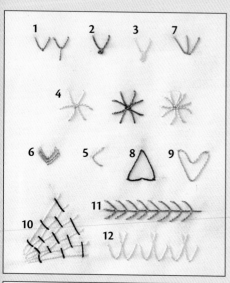

Fly Stitches

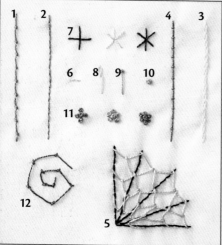

Knotted and Straight Stitches

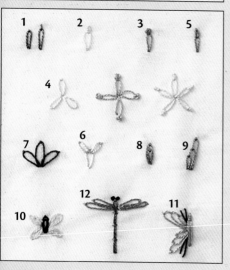

Lazy Daisy Stitches

Wrapped, Whipped, and Covered Stitches

1. Bullion Stitch (page 138)

2. Bullion Stitch Loop (page 138)

3. Bullion Stitch Rose (page 138)

4. Bullion Stitch Daisy (page 138)

5. Whip-Stitch Star (page 138)

6. Jill's Flower Stitch (page 138)

7. Jess's Flower Stitch (page 139)

8. Tiny Dragonfly Stitch (page 139)

9. Barnacle Stitch (page 139)

10. Gwen's Rose Stitch (page 139)

11. Frilled Petal Stitch (page 139)

12. Frilled Leaf Stitch (page 139)

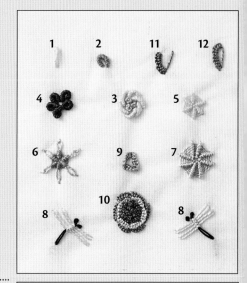

Silk Ribbon Embroidery Stitches

1. Ribbon Stitch (page 141)

2. Ribbon Loop Stitch (page 141)

3. Pointed Petal Stitch (page 141)

4. Silk Ribbon Flower Stitch (page 141)

5. Mum Stitch (page 141)

6. Whipped Stitch (page 142)

7. Whipped Posy Stitch (page 142)

8. Whipped Rose Stitch (page 142)

9. Woven Rose Stitch (page 142)

10. Pin Rose Stitch (page 142)

11. Accordion Rose Stitch (page 142)

12. Elegant Butterfly Stitch (page 142)

Bead Embroidery Stitches

1. Single Bead Stitch (page 144)

2. Grouped Bead Stitch (page 144)

3. Bead Combination Stitch (page 144)

4. Stacked Bead Stitch (page 144)

5. Picot Tip Stitch (page 144)

6. Bead Cascade Stitch (page 144)

7. Beaded Stamen Stitch (page 145)

8. Stem and Flower Stitch (page 145)

9. Continuous Bead Stitch (page 145)

10. Beaded Charms (page 145)

11. Top-to-Bottom Hole Charms (page 145)

12. Side-to-Side Hole Charms (page 145)

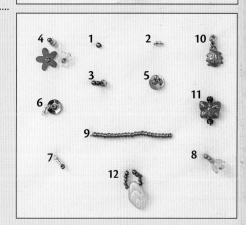

Embroidered Buttons

1. Stitched Buttons (page 147)

2. Stitched Buttons Fancy (page 147)

3. Embroidered Buttons: Lazy Daisy Stitch (page 147)

4. Embroidered Buttons: French Knot Stitch (page 147)

5. Embroidered Buttons: Fly Stitch (page 147)

6. Embroidered Buttons: Blanket Stitch (page 147)

7. Embroidered Buttons: Chain Stitch (page 147)

8. Stacked Buttons (page 147)

9. Clustered Buttons (page 147)

10. Button Spider (page 147)

11. Button Flower (page 147)

12. Beaded Buttons (page 147)

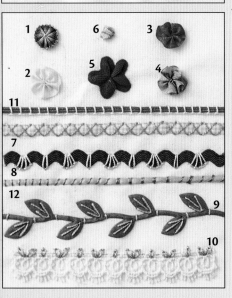

Ribbonwork Flowers and Trimmed Trims

1. Rosette (page 149)

2. Double Rosette (page 149)

3. Ribbon Posy (page 149)

4. Old Rose (page 150)

5. Rickrack Flower (page 150)

6. Detail Flower (page 150)

7. Ribbon Trim (page 151)

8. Rickrack Trim (page 151)

9. Leaf Trim (page 151)

10. Lace Trim (page 151)

11. Soutache Trim (page 151)

12. Rayon Cord Trim (page 151)

A STITCH BEYOND TIME

Embroidery Beginnings

Detail of my vintage quilt made by Mrs. Olson

At an early age I fell in love with fiber, quilts, clothing, and dolls. My bed was covered with stuffed animals that my mom had made. The bedcover, a hand-pieced crazy quilt by Mrs. Olson (a neighbor of my grandmother), was made from fabulous 1950s fabrics. I came to love the colors and shapes within the printed fabrics. The embroidery stitches worked on the quilt were simple and perfect.

I was just seven years old when I first learned to embroider. It was the first needle art that I learned, and it continues to be a favorite pastime. For my birthday that year, I was given a small sewing basket that I filled with skeins of floss, as well as bits of precious ribbon, lace, sequins, and beads. I worked my magic on little pieces of felt that I turned into clothes for my troll doll.

VINTAGE STITCHES

Throughout the years, many generations of women in my family have cherished embroidered items. Everyday household items like table-cloths, linens, and towels were commonplace in our house when I was a girl. Embroidery even found its way into the greeting cards my mom

Embroidered greeting cards

made. My mom did the cross-stitch work on the card to the right; the embroidered card on the left was found in my grandmother's keepsake drawer.

Fancier items like handkerchiefs and handbags were also treasured, each kept safe in its own little box on a shelf in the linen closet. The handbag on the left belonged to my grandmother. Its hand-embroidered satin stitch design was worked in silk threads on a brown bengaline

Embroidered handbags

background. The little black satin handbag belonged to my mother. Its embroidered chain stitches were done in a rayon thread with a tambour needle.

STITCHES IN SCHOOL

In high school I traded my embroidery skills for the creative skills of my friends. I embroidered work shirts and jeans, and in return they made me ceramic pots or jewelry.

In college I used my embroidery skills on the cover of a report I had written. The assignment was to write about a clothing brand or company that you liked or identified with. At the time I loved to go to Judy's, a store in our local mall that concentrated on the younger market.

Judy's

RESCUED STITCHES

Small embroidered bags and appliqué

Donna Reed's Tea Party

I have collected many embroidered textiles throughout the years, some purchased and some bequeathed. Whenever I find a discarded embroidered hanky or table runner at the thrift store, I wonder who made the item and why the family didn't keep it as an heirloom. The two small jewelry bags were embroidered entirely in silk ribbon. The appliqué was worked in a counted cross-stitch in silk threads on a solid silk fabric background.

I made this jacket from quite a few found treasures. I started with an appliquéd and embroidered tablecloth that had had a "run-in" with a bottle of Merlot wine. Though much of the white area had been ruined, the appliquéd areas had not. I cut around these areas and combined those sections with another tablecloth, many hankies, a few table runners, ribbons, buttons, and lots and lots of embroidery.

ALL THE RIGHT STUFF

1. Fabric	**4.** Stabilizers	**7.** Ribbons
2. Felt	**5.** Lace	**8.** Cords, trims, and braids
3. Silk roving	**6.** Appliqués	**9.** Floss

10. Perle cotton	**13.** Seed beads
11. Metallic thread	**14.** Buttons
12. Silk embroidery ribbon	**15.** Sequins

16. Charms
17. Found objects

Getting Started

The design and construction of a project should be reflected in the fabrics, trims, ribbons, laces, embroidery threads, beads, and other components that you choose to work with. See Design Basics (page 36) for further information.

Fabrics

Solid fabrics in cotton, batiste, denim, linen, moiré, wool, and silk are suitable, as are cotton prints, hand-dyed fabrics, and batik fabrics. Other base materials, such as felt squares and silk roving, can be interesting to work with. Keep in mind that some amount of fabric will show through the embroidery stitches; therefore, you don't want the fabric's color or pattern to overpower the embroidered design and vice versa. Once you choose your fabrics, you can decide whether to make a wholecloth or pieced base.

Sand Pebbles, linen fabric with appliquéd lace doily

Melted Crayons, silk fabrics crazy pieced into squares with a strip-pieced border

Stabilizers

I suggest using some form of stabilizer for the backing of any project while embroidering; this will minimize the wrinkling and distortion of the fabrics as you stitch. If you desire a firmer base once you have completed the embroidery, use batting or something heavier (such as fast2fuse or Timtex interfacing) during the assembly process.

Tatiana's Garden, solid piece of cotton fabric with vintage lace sections formed into a basket with a handle; backed with fast2fuse

Blue Heart Etui, modified version of log cabin piecing using two large print fabrics; backed with Timtex

Lace and Appliqués

You can use lace yardage and appliqués as part of a pieced design or as a shape to embroider around. New and vintage laces can be found in a variety of widths, styles, and fiber contents. Lace yardage can be backed with fabric and stitched as one piece of fabric. Lace trims should be hand stitched onto the project first with sewing thread, and then embroidered on or around the edges.

Detail of *Midnight in Paris* (full photo on page 84): crazy-pieced cotton, dyed silk fabric, and vintage lace yardage; lace and ribbons dyed with COLORHUE dyes

Detail of *Spring Butterflies* (full photo on page 97): strip-pieced silk fabric with the embroidery worked off of the vintage butterfly appliqués and lace trim

Ribbons

Satin, jacquard, grosgrain, and velvet ribbons can be stitched onto the project by machine or by hand. Embroidery stitches can be worked on the selvage edges or down the center of a solid-colored ribbon. Ribbons can also be used for ribbonwork flowers and trimmed trims (page 148) or as a functional part of the design by covering the raw edges of two adjacent seams.

Detail of *Lady Bird 2* (full photo on page 83): cotton fabrics with woven ribbons and lace yardage

Cords, Trims, and Braids

You can hand stitch rattail or mouse-tail rayon cords, soutache, or braids to fabric, whether following a shape or creating a shape to embroider around. Cords, trims, or braids can be couched or stitched in place with an embroidery stitch using threads or beads. These trims can also be applied to the outer edges of the finished base to add extra interest.

Detail of *Jelly Beans* (full photo on page 62): appliquéd felt with soutache braids

Embroidery Threads and Ribbons

Embroidery threads come in a variety of materials, weights, and colors, in both twisted and flat threads. The choice of thread should be determined by the embroidery stitches and your overall design. Silk ribbon made especially for embroidery comes in a variety of sizes.

FLOSS

Floss is a flat six-stranded thread that comes wrapped in a skein. A variety of fiber contents are available, including cotton, linen, silk, and rayon. Cotton and silk can be found in solid, ombré, variegated, and hand-dyed colors. Linen floss and rayon floss can be found in solid colors.

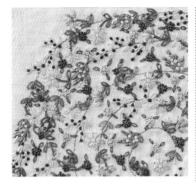

Detail of *Merrily We Go Around* (full photo on page 67): embroidered with seventeen colors of cotton floss

TWISTED THREADS

Perle cotton and silk perle threads give stitches some dimension. Perle cotton is a two-ply twisted cotton thread that comes in a skein or a ball; it is available in a variety of solid, ombré, variegated, and hand-dyed colors. I recommend sizes #5, #8, #10, or #12 for the embroidery stitches in this book. Specialty threads can be found in hand-dyed and solid colors. Two examples are Wildflowers thread, which is perle cotton #12, and Subtlety, which is a silk perle found in size #12.

Detail of *Chrysanthemum Tea* (full photo on page 94): embroidered with perle cotton and cotton floss

METALLIC THREADS

Metallic threads come in a variety of styles and sizes, including floss, twisted threads, cords, and ribbon. These threads can be found in a variety of metallic colors, such as gold, silver, and copper, in addition to other solid colors, such as red, blue, purple, black, and green.

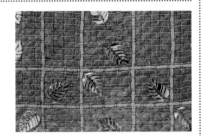

Detail of *Enmeshed* (full photo on page 93): silk fiber with vintage metallic mesh and embroidered with metallic threads and sequins

SILK EMBROIDERY RIBBON

Ribbons that are made especially for silk embroidery have a woven edge. This ribbon is sold by the yard or on cards, spools, or plastic reels. The most popular sizes are 2 mm, 4 mm, and 7 mm, though 13 mm and wider can occasionally be found.

Detail of *Cancun Dreams* (full photo on page 110): hand-dyed silk fabric embroidered with hand-dyed 4 mm and 7 mm silk embroidery ribbon

Embellishments

Beads, buttons, charms, and found objects can add a personal touch to any project. Often these little extras give the project an identity that is unique to your own style while helping to tell the project's story.

BEADS

Beads come in many different shapes and sizes. The colors and finishes available are almost as extensive as the variety of threads and ribbons.

Detail of *Mystic Twilight* (full photo on page 99): embellished with vintage glass buttons and glass beads

BUTTONS

Buttons also come in a variety of materials, shapes, and sizes. Sew-through buttons can be stitched to the fabric base with an embroidery stitch using thread or beads; see Embroidered Buttons (page 146) for more ideas. Shank buttons can be stitched to the fabric base with sewing or embroidery thread.

Detail of *Bouncing Button Balloons* (full photo on page 51): embellished with vintage celluloid and cloth buttons and seed beads

SEQUINS

Sequins are available in a variety of shapes, colors, finishes, and sizes. They usually have a center hole to attach them to fabric. Sequins can be stitched into the center of a flower or to an embroidered row of stitches to add a bit of unexpected color and sparkle.

Detail of *Harlequin Peacock* (full photo on page 74): embellished with vintage and new sequins and seed beads

CHARMS AND FOUND OBJECTS

Charms come in a variety of shapes, colors, finishes, and sizes. They usually have a hole placed in the center, through the center, or to the side of the shape. Any found object with a hole can be attached with sewing thread, embroidery thread, silk ribbon, or a group of beads. Items that do not have a hole can be glued in place.

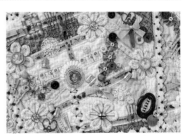

Detail of *Scraps and Leftovers* (full photo on page 94): embellished with ribbons, trims, zippers, lace, charms, buttons, buckles, snaps, safety pins, clothespins, and more

COLOR THEORY 101

Color Board

The color board is a basic tool to help you identify color families and see how the colors fall within those families. This board consists of 60 solid colors of fabric, thread, and beads digitally derived from 5 basic gray-scale models. I have used these to illustrate the topics within this chapter.

Hue/color family	Red	Red/orange	Orange	Yellow/orange	Yellow	Yellow/green
Dark						
Medium/dark						
Medium						
Medium/light						
Light						

note

- The colors that fall within the same vertical column are called a color hue or family.

- The colors descending from dark to light in the vertical column are defined as a tint or shade.

- The colors that fall within the same horizontal row are all the same value: tint, shade, or tone.

Green	Blue/green	Blue	Blue/violet	Violet	Red/violet	Hue/color family
						Dark
						Medium/dark
						Medium
						Medium/light
						Light

THE COLORS

Primary Colors

Red, yellow, blue. These are true colors that have not been combined with any other hue to create the color.

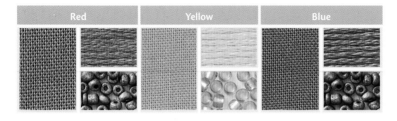

Secondary Colors

Orange, green, violet. These colors are a mix of equal parts of two primary hues.

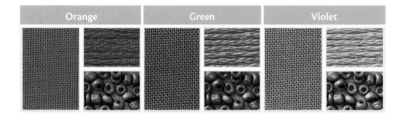

Tertiary Colors

Red/orange, yellow/orange, yellow/green, blue/green, blue/violet, red/violet. These colors are a mix of two primary hues. The primary color at the beginning of the color name is used in a stronger amount than the second hue in the name.

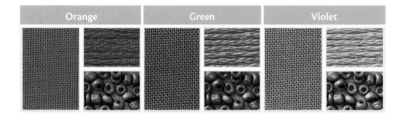

DEFINING THE COLORS

Hue: the pure color (medium)

Tint: the pure color with white added (light)

Shade: the pure color with black added (dark)

Tone: the pure color with gray added (medium light or medium dark)

Warm color: red/violet, red, red/orange, orange, yellow/orange, yellow

Cool color: yellow/green, green, blue/green, blue, blue/violet, violet

Finding Harmony

To help you get started in choosing a palette, I have listed a few color theories or harmonies, many with which you may already be familiar.

COMPLEMENTARY HARMONY

One primary hue and one secondary hue

Red and green   Yellow and violet   Blue and orange

MONOCHROMATIC HARMONY

Two or more values within the same hue

Red/violet

ANALOGOUS HARMONY

Two or three hues of any value that lie next to each other on the color board

Green   Blue/green   Blue

SPLIT-COMPLEMENTARY HARMONY

Three hues of any value—one hue and the two colors on either side of the complementary color of the first hue

Red   Blue/green   Yellow/green

TRIAD HARMONY

Three hues of any value that are equally spaced from each other

Red/orange   Yellow/green   Blue/violet

TETRAD HARMONY

Four or more hues of any value that are equally spaced from each other

Red   Yellow   Green   Violet

Gallery Examples

Here are some examples of how I used the color harmonies (previous page) in choosing my palette. Sometimes they were just a starting point to which I added other colors or neutrals. In the descriptions below, I chose to use familiar names for the colors.

Detail of *For Elizabeth* (full photo on page 105): split-complementary color harmony of fuchsia, green, and violet, with white added as a neutral color

Detail of *My Crazy Valentine* (full photo on page 59): complementary color harmony of red and green, with cream added as a neutral color

Detail of *Batik Galaxy* (full photo on page 55): triad color harmony of cranberry, mustard, and turquoise blue (slight variation)

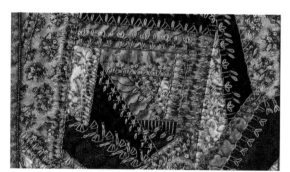

Detail of *Purple Haze* (full photo on page 46): monochromatic color harmony of purple

Detail of *Blue Lilies* (full photo on page 95): analogous color harmony of blue/green, blue, and blue/violet

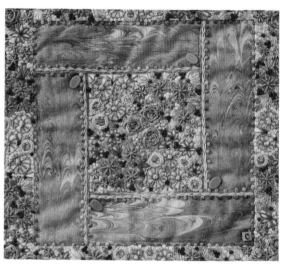

Detail of *California Dreamin'* (full photo on page 103): tetrad color harmony of red, orange, yellow, green, blue, and violet

Choosing a Color Palette

The color palette can begin with the fabric that will be used for the base of your project or perhaps a variegated thread with many colors to choose from. When choosing fabrics, you can work with any of the previous color suggestions or any of the color discipline suggestions in Colorful Creations (page 45).

If you decide to work with your own color palette, I suggest starting with colors that you like so that the first need will be met. You can choose to work within one hue or family, choose several hues that are all the same value, or choose several hues and a variety of values. The number of colors—whether solid or print—is up to you. The main thing to work toward is a balance of color.

PALETTE EXAMPLE

Once you have the basic palette, you can choose the threads, ribbons, trims, laces, and embellishments. These can be in the same hue and value as the fabric or in a lighter or darker value. In the following example, I chose the fabric in the medium value, the thread in the light value, and the beads in the dark value; again, the main thing to work toward is a balance of color.

COLOR PALETTE RECIPE

I create a color palette by first placing the fabrics next to each other as they would appear in the pieced base. Then I assign the fabrics a corresponding number and name. If I am working with a solid background, I place the threads as they would be used and give them a number and name. All of the remaining components that are the same color are labeled with the same name and number as the fabric or embroidery components. If more colors are added in—whether they are fabrics, trims, or thread—they will be given a corresponding number and name.

I then create a chart, using the numbers and names of the fabrics, and then I list the categories in which these colors will be used. (See the chart, page 24, for an example.) I call this the embroider-by-number chart.

TRIAD HARMONY

Components		Orange		Green		Violet	
Fabric	Thread						
	Beads						

Color and Embroidery Example

The beauty of the embroider-by-number chart is that the colors will continue to flow around the pieced base, so you never have to guess what color should be used where! Here is an example of an embroider-by-number chart.

EMBROIDER-BY-NUMBER CHART

Fabric	Blue 1	Orange 2	Purple 3	Green 4	Red 5
Border row	Orange 2	Purple 3	Green 4	Red 5	Blue 1
Decorative stitches	Purple 3	Green 4	Red 5	Blue 1	Orange 2
Detail stitches	Green 4	Red 5	Blue 1	Orange 2	Purple 3
Beads and embellishments	Red 5	Blue 1	Orange 2	Purple 3	Green 4

Here is an example of how the colors will flow in a project using the embroider-by-number chart. The fabrics were chosen in medium colors, the threads in medium/dark colors.

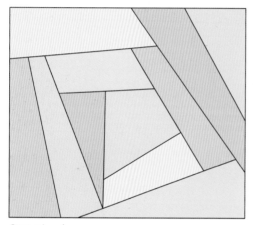

Crazy-pieced square

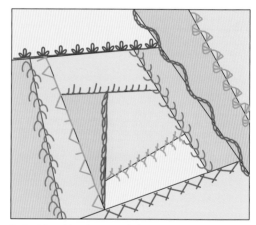

Embroidered border row stitches

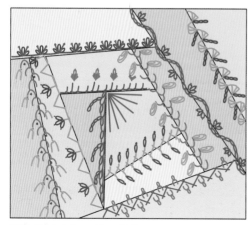

Embroidered decorative stitches

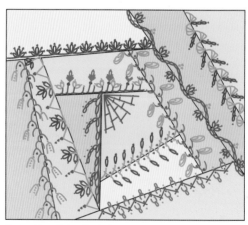

Embroidered detail stitches

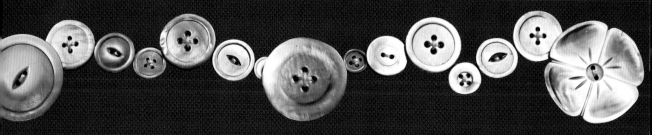

DESIGNING A PROJECT

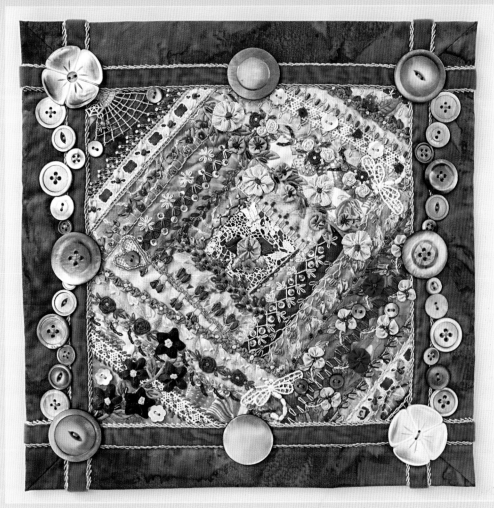

Crazy Lady

My favorite projects are those that combine a variety of materials, threads, ribbons, beads, and embellishments. This small patch of crazy-pieced cotton and lace fabrics is one of those projects. The embroidery and embellishments include ribbonwork flowers, vintage appliqués, silk embroidery ribbon, perle cotton, floss, beads, buttons, sequins, and charms. I stitched vintage buttons along a bordered frame trimmed with velvet ribbon and embroidered with perle cotton.

Where Do Ideas Come From?

Often I build a piece around a special object, such as a family heirloom or a gift from a family member or friend. For you, this could be a special button, a strand of vintage beads, or perhaps a piece of lace that you want to feature in a project.

Charmed Square, nine-patch square of cotton fabrics: This project's color inspiration came from a brooch that I made using vintage buttons and earrings.

Project Development

When I gather components for a project, I start with color first. The inspiration can come from a favorite fabric, a button, or a spool of special thread. Once I have an idea for the color palette, I set aside a box or space on my worktable and begin pulling components from my stash.

For Elizabeth, vintage batiste handkerchief purchased at a thrift store for $1.00: The theme came together with lace appliqués and ribbonwork flowers that were left over from another project.

A key factor to any project is the level of commitment and cost you are willing to put into it. Some projects can be made with very few components or expense, while others may require more.

Key Elements

Once I have gathered all the components, the thought process begins. If there is an unlimited supply of each component, then the project has many possibilities. However, if there is a limited supply of fabric or embellishments, this has to be taken into consideration.

Whether the design is to be simple or complex, the following six key elements determine the look and feel of the finished project:

- Theme
- Color
- Fabric
- Construction
- Embroidery design
- Embroidery materials and embellishments

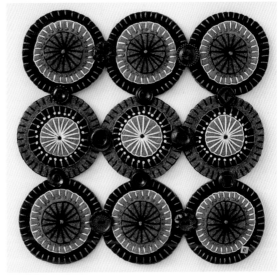

Shades of Gray, felt penny rug made from inexpensive materials, synthetic felt, and cotton floss

THEME

Each project has its own personality or theme. When I begin a project, I give it a name. Sometimes this is simply the name of the fabric. A more complex title may come from a favorite family member. However you choose to determine the theme, it should be reflected through every step of the design process—from the color choices to the construction, to the embroidery design, and to the threads and embellishments you choose.

Lady Bird's Bzzy Garden, crazy-pieced cotton fabrics: The overall design came from the two print fabrics with flowers and ladybugs.

COLOR

If you are not sure where to start, I suggest beginning with a print or piece of dyed fabric that you like; then choose the colors from within that print for additional fabrics and other components you want to use. Another idea is to start with your favorite colors or a palette that works in your home. For further inspiration, see Color Theory 101 (page 18) and Colorful Creations (page 45).

Detail of *Fireworks* (full photo on page 90): The colors for this project came from the printed felt square and variegated cotton floss in the same colors.

Accent Colors

It is perfectly acceptable to include additional colors of threads, beads, or other components that are not in your original color palette. Simply adding black or white to a project can create a dramatic effect.

Another suggestion is to add a metallic color such as gold, silver, or copper to give the project a bit of sparkle. I suggest using the following metallic colors on the suggested tints and shades.

Gold: use it on fabrics that have a warm tint.

Antique gold: use it on fabrics that have a warm shade.

Silver: use it on fabrics that have a cool tint.

Antique silver: use it on fabrics that have a cool shade.

Copper: use it on fabrics that have a cool tone.

Antique copper: use it on fabrics that have a warm tone.

FABRIC

Whatever your fabric choice, the weave and content will certainly lend a great deal to the project's design. For a homespun look, choose denim, muslin, or quaint cotton prints; for a more sophisticated look, choose silks or moiré fabrics and vintage lace. For a contemporary look, try batiks or hand-dyed fabrics.

Ribbon-embroidered brooches: The fabrics, colors, and additional trims changed the look and feel of the simple embroidered design.

CONSTRUCTION

The construction of the fabric base will determine the overall embroidery and embellishment design. The fabric base can be a whole cloth, a simple strip-pieced construction, or a more complicated base with appliqués. Once the base is pieced, the embroidery design will follow.

Whole Cloth

I suggest using a machine-stitched or machine-quilted pattern to break up a wholecloth background and to give the embroidery stitches a path to follow. Additional elements such as ribbons, laces, or other trims will add more possibilities for the embroidered and embellished designs.

Appliqué

An appliqué can be a lace doily or a fabric shape that is applied to the fabric base. A reverse appliqué technique can be used where the fabric base is cut into a shape; then another piece of fabric can be placed under the opening.

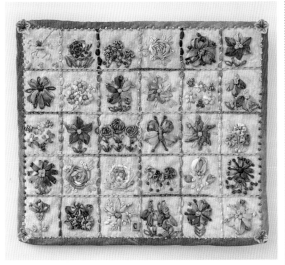

Flower Child, solid piece of dyed silk fabric: A grid of couched floss and ribbon creates sections for the embroidered stitches.

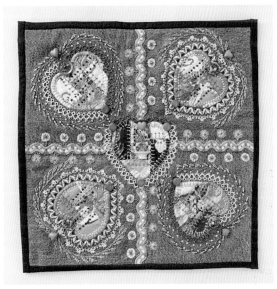

Country Hearts, pieced appliqués stitched onto a denim background

Pieced

A pieced design can be as simple or complicated as you want. A simple base may use additional trims to bring in a design element; a more complex base can rely on the intricacy of the piecing.

Charlotte's Webs, crazy-pieced silk fabrics with ribbon trim

EMBROIDERY DESIGN

The embroidery design is determined by the construction of the fabrics and other materials you choose to include in the design. The fabric base is the first consideration. The second consideration is the placement of any large embellishment components, such as an appliqué, large button, or other item. In Embroider, Embellish, and Explore (page 78), I provide several different design suggestions.

Whole Cloth

The embroidery design can follow a pattern in a printed fabric, a machine-stitched line, or a hand-embroidered cord. (See Bordered Designs, page 101.) The embroidery design can be stitched into small groups or stitched to create a larger design. (See Bordered Designs, page 101, and Overall Design, page 109.)

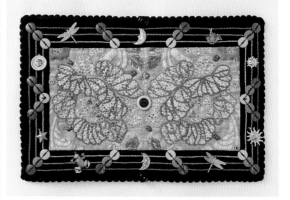

Santa Fe Summer: The embroidered design follows the print of the fabric, with bordered rows on the outer edges.

Appliqué

An appliquéd design can be followed with embroidery and embellishments. (See Appliqué Embroidery, page 89.) Or the appliqué can be the focal point from which all the embroidery stems. (See Shadow Embroidery, page 97.)

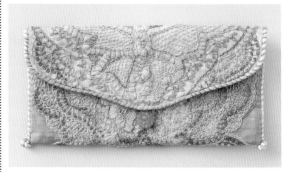

Spring Butterflies, strip-pieced silk fabric with the embroidery worked off of the butterfly appliqués and lace strip sections

Pieced

The base can be a simple strip-pieced base or a more complicated crazy-pieced base. The design will be determined by how much space you have for each piece of fabric or seam. It will also depend on whether any extra elements, such as trims, lace, small appliqué shapes, or buttons, are added.

Lady Bird 2, crazy-pieced base with embroidery worked off the seams, over several seams, and in the center of the larger fabric shapes

EMBROIDERY MATERIALS

The embroidery materials you choose will determine the stitches and other techniques you can use for the embroidered design. If the fabrics have a print or pattern, choose one type of thread or color for the embroidery stitches; this will add design details without competing with the design of the fabric or base. If the fabrics are a solid color or a muted batik, a variety of threads and colors can be used to enhance and create a rich, interesting look. See the embroidery and embellishment stitch reference guide (page 114) for further details.

Perle Cotton and Cotton Floss

Perle cotton and cotton floss are very versatile materials that can be worked on most fabrics.

Rasta Pincushion, embroidered with cotton floss

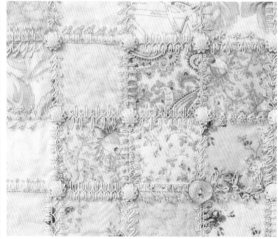

Detail of *Paris Flea Market* (full photo on page 80): nine-patch charm squares embroidered with perle cotton

Silk Threads and Silk Embroidery Ribbon

The silk floss and perles can be worked in the same stitches as their cotton counterparts. Silk embroidery ribbon can be worked in these stitches or in stitches that are designed specifically for silk embroidery ribbon.

Detail of *Blue Lilies* (full photo on page 95): embroidered with silk embroidery ribbon, silk perle, and cotton floss

Embellishments

Embellishments such as charms, beads, buttons, or found objects can give a different dimension to a project. For ideas on which metallic colors look best on which fabric colors, see Accent Colors (page 28).

 note

If the beads, buttons, and charms are to be used as accents, it is not necessary to use them in every color of your chosen palette.

Fields of Gold: The center is an antique porcelain button given to me by a student; additional embellishments include vintage and new buttons, silk embroidery ribbons, and perle cotton.

Finishing Touches

Once you have finished the embroidery and embellishments but before you have assembled the base, there are still a few things you can do to make your project special.

BINDING OPTIONS

Adding a pieced or wide binding creates a frame that can be further embellished. Adding objects after sewing the binding can also create interest.

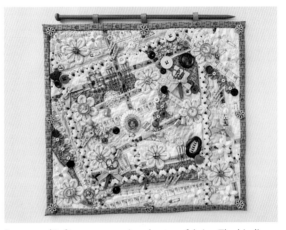

Scraps and Leftovers, crazy-pieced cotton fabrics: The binding was embellished with buttons. Ribbon loops support the wooden knitting needle. In addition, the lining has a crazy-pieced pocket that holds a special object.

Paris Flea Market, nine-patch charm squares bordered with muslin fabric: Mother-of-pearl buttons were stitched around the wide outer border muslin fabric.

TRIMMED EDGES

Additional trims such as silk rouleaux, ribbons, or cords can be stitched to the finished base; ribbons can also be used to create a frame.

Sweet Roses and Posies, embroidered with silk embroidery ribbon and perle cotton: Silk rouleau was hand couched around the outer edge with perle cotton.

50s Flashback, crazy pieced with cotton fabrics: Vintage jacquard and grosgrain ribbons create the border and frame; rayon cord was hand couched around the frame.

UNEXPECTED ADDITIONS

Additional objects such as vintage purse handles or old keys can easily be stitched or glued in place. These unexpected treasures can be stitched around the finished project or used for the hanger.

Crème de la Crème, crazy-pieced lace: The finished edge was couched with silk rouleau. Two sets of vintage bone purse handles create the border around the outer edge of the fabric base.

Rustic Door, pieced batik fabrics with appliqué door: Ribbon creates a border, adding more of the midnight blue color. A vintage key hangs from moiré ribbon, creating a unique hanger.

FOUND OBJECTS

Found objects such as small frames can be used to border a design within the project. New and old jewelry findings can be used to showcase small pieces, such as old watch casings or jewelry parts.

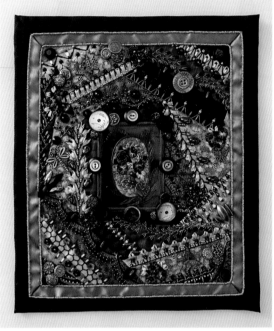

Midnight in Paris, crazy-pieced cotton, dyed silk, and vintage lace yardage: An antique metal frame borders the center vignette. A border of ribbon embellished with beads creates an inner frame within the fabric outer frame for the project.

Bracelet made from grosgrain ribbon, silk embroidery ribbon, old buttons, and vintage watchcase; new watch fob with embroidered center; and old diamanté pin back with embroidered center

FLYING NEEDLES

Victoriana, side 1

a special note

I really feel that the art of embroidery should be enjoyed, and the best way to do this is to be confident with your stitching techniques. Perfection is not something that I insist you strive for, but a familiarity with the stitches will make you feel more confident when creating and stitching your own designs.

Allowing yourself to learn and experiment with a new technique is never a waste of time. Understanding the basic stitches with each variation or derivative will prepare you for your journey into embroidery. May that be a long enjoyable journey, and may your needles fly!

Design Basics

A few of the pieces that I have included in this book use the same fabrics or design, but each has a very different look. Compare the groups below for ideas.

I used the same printed fabrics for each wallhanging (at right). On *Lady Bird's Bzzy Garden*, I used black as an accent color. The color discipline was Follow the Leader (page 74). On *Lady Bird 2*, I used cream as an accent color. The color discipline was Colors and More Colors (page 66).

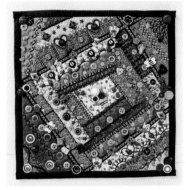

Lady Bird's Bzzy Garden, crazy-pieced embroidery and vignette designs using the color discipline Follow the Leader

Lady Bird 2, bordered design, vignette designs, and crazy-pieced embroidery using the color discipline Colors and More Colors

These examples of the same wool felt appliquéd shapes (at right) show different amounts of embroidery and embellishments. For the first group, I used cotton floss for the embroidery with quite a few embellishments. For the wallhanging, I chose perle cotton for the simple border row and detail stitches.

Country Hearts, appliqué embroidery

50s Flashback, crazy-pieced embroidery and vignette designs

The pieced appliqué shapes in *Country Hearts* were made from three of the same prints used in the crazy-pieced base of *50s Flashback* (bottom left). I used perle cotton to embroider the first piece and a combination of perle cotton, silk embroidery ribbon, and cotton floss for the second.

Group of felt appliqués, straight-seam embroidery

Photo by Barbara Donahay

The Village Sleeps Tonight, straight-seam embroidery

Defining a Stitch

The embroidery stitches listed in the embroidery and embellishment stitch reference guide (page 114) are presented as a family of stitches that can be one stitch and its variations or several similar stitches. These are presented as border row or detail stitches. In this chapter, the use of these stitches is further explained. See The Basics (page 152) for tools, needle sizes, and other tips.

BORDER ROW STITCHES

Border row stitches are worked in a continuous row along a straight or curved line. These stitches can be a continuous stitch or a group of decorative stitches stitched along a row. Border row stitches can also be worked as one of the design components of a vignette.

Blanket stitch (page 116)

Chain stitch (page 120)

Feather stitch (page 126)

INDIVIDUAL STITCHES

Decorative and detail stitches are a single unit that can be worked individually on the tip or on open sections of a border row, worked into a vignette, or used to fill in entire sections of fabric.

Decorative Stitches

Bullion stitch (page 138)

Lazy daisy stitch (page 135)

Heart stitch (page 130)

Detail Stitches

French knot stitch (page 133)

Straight stitch (page 132)

Single bead stitch (page 144)

SHAPES AND COMPOSITE STITCHES

A single stitch can be grouped and repeated side by side or into a circle to create a shape or larger component. A composite stitch is comprised of one or more individual stitches worked to create a larger component. These stitches can be worked onto a border row, into a vignette, or to fill in entire sections of fabric.

Grouped Individual Stitches

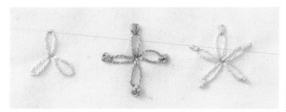

Lazy daisy stitch flower (page 135)

Silk ribbon flower stitch (page 141)

Fly stitch stacked (page 129)

Composite Stitches

Butterfly stitch (page 136)

Tiny dragonfly stitch (page 139)

Button spider (page 147)

Working the Stitches

At the beginning of each stitch family is a list of the recommended materials best suited for those stitches. You can work individual stitches alone or in groups, following the design or pattern; when the design is complete, knot and cut the thread. Work the border row stitches to the end of the row or pattern, and then knot and cut the thread. If at some point you need to add thread, see Adding Thread (page 40) for suggestions.

STITCH DIRECTION

When embroidering the border row, individual, and detail stitches, keep the direction of the stitches in mind. The direction in which the stitch should be worked in a vignette is based on the design. For instance, the chain stitch can be worked in any direction out from a design, but the feather stitch is started away from a design and worked toward it.

When embroidery is worked on a seam detail, the design is determined by where the seam is placed relative to the project's overall shape. This, of course, can be left to your own discretion.

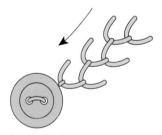

Feather stitch worked into a vignette

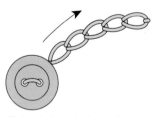

Chain stitch worked out of a vignette

STITCH LENGTH

The stitch length should directly correlate to the size of the thread or ribbon you are using. In general, take a smaller stitch when using a fine thread or fewer strands of floss; take a larger stitch for heavier threads or for more strands of floss. The same theory applies to the size of silk embroidery ribbon. Take a smaller stitch with 2 mm silk ribbon than with 7 mm silk ribbon.

Variations in Length

Changing the distance between **A**, **B**, and **C** can vary the shape of the fly stitch (page 129) and the feather stitch (page 126).

At the left, the spacing between **A**, **B**, and **C** is equal. At the center, **A** and **B** are closer, and **C** is farther apart. At the right, **A** and **B** are farther apart, and **C** is closer.

Variations in Stitch Technique

When stitching around an appliqué shape, button, or trim, it is easier to perform a stitch like the chain stitch in three strokes—up, down, up—rather than in two strokes.

1. Come up at **A**.
2. Go down at **B**, pulling the thread slightly to form the stitch.
3. Come up at **C**, pulling the thread all the way through.

ADDING THREAD

Looped Stitches: Feather, Buttonhole, or Chain Stitch

Straight Stitches: Outline or Back Stitch

1. Knot and cut the old thread after **B**; start the new thread at **C**.

1. Stitch **B** of a looped stitch down through the fabric, but do not pull the thread taut. Stitch a new thread through the loop at **C**. Pull the old thread to form the loop.

2. Stitch 1 or 2 stitches with the new thread; then knot and cut the old thread. Continue to stitch with the new thread.

What, Where, When?

I think it helps to have an idea of where the colors are going to be used—see Color and Embroidery Example (page 24); Colorful Creations (page 45); and Embroider, Embellish, and Explore (page 78).

EMBROIDERY STITCHES AND MATERIALS

The materials you choose will, of course, depend on the project's overall design. Here are some simple examples. For suggestions on materials, see All the Right Stuff (page 13).

EMBROIDERED ROWS

Border row stitches	Decorative stitches	Detail stitches
Choice 1		
Perle cotton #8	Perle cotton #8	Perle cotton #8
Choice 2		
Perle cotton #8	3 strands of cotton floss	Size 11 seed beads
Choice 3		
Perle cotton #8	Perle cotton #12	3 strands of cotton floss
Choice 4		
Perle cotton #12	3 strands of cotton floss	2 strands of cotton floss

VIGNETTES

Large components	Medium components	Small components	Detail stitches
Choice 1			
7mm silk embroidery ribbon	4mm silk embroidery ribbon	Perle cotton #8	Perle cotton #12
Choice 2			
4mm silk embroidery ribbon	2mm silk embroidery ribbon	Perle cotton #8	3 strands of cotton floss
Choice 3			
Perle cotton #8	Perle cotton #12	3 strands of cotton floss	Size 11 seed beads

EMBROIDERY AS A SEAM TREATMENT

The size of the seam and the section of fabric before the next seam will determine the size of the embroidered row and its components. The border row can be stitched on one side of the seam, or it can straddle a seam. The decorative and detail stitches can be worked on either side of the seam.

Straight- and Crazy-Pieced Seams

Victoriana, side 2 (See page 114 for a larger photo.)

If the embroidered row design is worked on a wide strip of fabric, choose a border row stitch that can be worked wider, such as the feather or blanket stitch. These stitches provide multiple opportunities for decorative and detail stitches. If the embroidered row design is worked on a smaller seam and section of fabric, consider using a narrower stitch like a chain or coral stitch, or consider stitching the embroidered row design to cover several seams.

Appliqué Shapes and Curved Seams

Fireworks (See page 90 for a larger photo.)

In this type of appliqué, the embroidery can be used for assembly purposes as well as decoration. The blanket, chain, and single feather stitch are good choices. For border row stitches around a circular shape or curved seam, choose a stitch that can easily be curved. Note that the edge of the stitch next to the shape will be shorter, and the tip will fan out, mirroring the shape.

Embroidered Trims

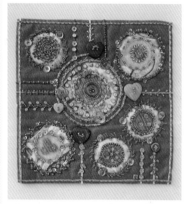

Jelly Beans (See page 62 for a larger photo.)

Any trim such as ribbon, lace, or cording should be stitched or glued in place to the fabric base first. Stitching can be done during the piecing process or afterward, either by machine or by hand. Keep in mind that the thread you use may show—so keep the stitches small and inconspicuous.

If the trim has a design like a leaf shape, consider using decorative and detail stitches on and around the leaves. If the trim has a straight edge, treat this as a straight seam and stitch an embroidered row off the edge. If the edge is shaped, work decorative and detail stitches off the tips of the shape.

EMBROIDERY AS A DESIGN ELEMENT

The embroidered design for a wholecloth base will either be an overall pattern or be worked with several smaller vignettes. Additional materials such as appliqué shapes, ribbons, trims, and buttons can be used to start or fill out the design.

Shadow Embroidery

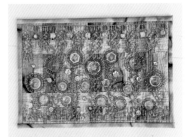

Mystic Twilight (See page 99 for a larger photo.)

Embroidery can be worked off or around a shape such as a button or an appliqué, with the stitches mirroring the shape. The embroidery will start at one section and then work around the shape back to the beginning stitch. If you are stitching around a button, choose a decorative stitch such as the lazy daisy stitch, which can be repeated starting at the center of the shank. If you are stitching around a flat button, choose a detail stitch such as the French knot. If you are working with an appliqué shape, choose a border row stitch that can easily be worked into the shape's edges or worked off of the shape, such as a blanket stitch or chain stitch.

Bordered Design

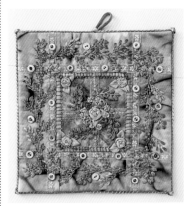

Sweet Roses and Posies (See page 102 for a larger photo.)

In a bordered design, the embroidery can mirror a seam, trim, or imaginary line. The line can be machine stitched or hand embroidered, or created with a ribbon or trim. In addition, whole sections of fabric can be filled with embroidery, while other sections can have minimal embroidery.

Vignette and Overall Designs

Charlotte's Webs (See page 107 for a larger photo.)

The embroidery stitches for a vignette or a large design should be worked in the following order: large components, medium components, small components, and detail stitches.

Embroidery Journal Project

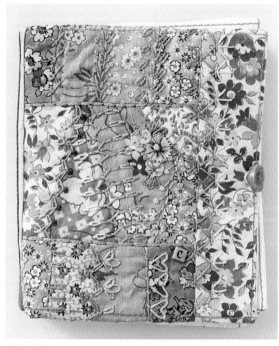

Embroidery Journal

UNFOLDED SIZE: 10″ × 5½″

Materials

¾ yard of solid-color background fabric for pages and cover

1 yard of lightweight iron-on interfacing

Variety of threads, ribbons, and beads

 note

Optional: Fabric scraps for pieced cover; button and 2½″ of ⅛″-wide satin ribbon for closure

DIRECTIONS

1. Cut 6 rectangles of fabric 10″ × 6″. Each piece will yield 2 pages, with 1 page per stitch family. Cut a rectangle of fabric 10½″ × 6″ for the cover.

2. Back each piece of fabric with lightweight interfacing, following the manufacturer's instructions.

3. Fold the length of the 10″ × 6″ pieces of fabric in half right sides together and press the center fold. Following the diagram, mark the outlines with a chalk pencil. Stitch each line with a running stitch, backstitch, or machine-stitched line.

4. Sampler pages: Embroider each page with a stitch family. (See Embroidery and Embellishment Stitch Reference Guide, page 114.)

5. Journal cover: Crazy piece or strip piece the base; embroider the seams with a variety of stitches. Follow the diagram in Step 3, marking the outer seams only, and then stitch. Fold under the top and bottom raw edges ¼″ to the wrong side; press.

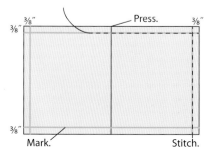

6. Working with a sampler page at a time, fold right sides together and press the center fold again. Stitch the fold with an ⅛" seam allowance; press flat. Fold under the top and bottom raw edges ¼" to the wrong side; press.

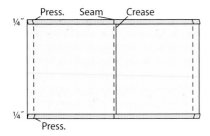

7. Place 2 sampler pages right sides together. Pin the right edge of the bottom piece to the left edge of the top piece. Machine stitch the raw edges together with a ¼" seam allowance. Press the seams open.

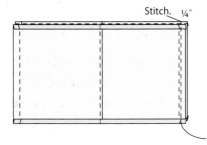

8. Follow Step 7 for the remaining sampler pages, with the right edge of the previous sampler page stitched to the left edge of the following page.

9. Pin the right edge of the cover to the left edge of the first sampler page, right sides together. Machine stitch the raw edges together with a ¼" seam allowance. Press the seams open. Repeat for the back of the cover and the last sampler page. See the tip (at right) to make the optional button loop closure.

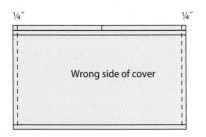

10. Pin the top edge of the journal cover to the first sampler page. Hand stitch the sections together with a whipstitch, beginning at the outer seam and sewing to the folded and stitched seam at the center. Repeat for the bottom edge. Repeat for each adjacent page. A small gap in the middle of the book will be created to form a binding for the spine of the book.

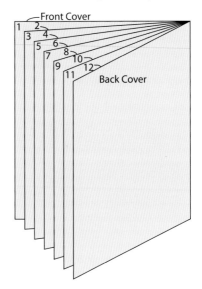

tip

Button loop option: In Step 9, fold the length of ribbon in half, pin, and stitch it to the back of the cover. Stitch the button to the front of the cover once the journal is finished.

COLORFUL CREATIONS

Mono y Mono, page 46

Double Down, page 50

Triple Delight, page 54

Four Square, page 58

Five and Dime, page 62

Colors and More Colors, page 66

Piggyback Jack, page 70

Follow the Leader, page 74

Color Disciplines

In the following pages, I provide examples of the eight different color disciplines that I use most often in my work. A number reference in the name of the discipline refers to the number of fabric or main component colors; the remaining disciplines refer to the choice of embroidery materials.

COLOR PALETTE CHART

Over the years I have developed an embroider-by-number chart (page 24) that I use on each project. This chart provides me with a set of guidelines to follow for the embroidery stitch and embellishment color placement. I jot down the chart on an index card and keep it with the project. I assure you that this has come in handy when I leave a project and come back after many months (or years!).

For further reading, see Color Theory 101 (page 18); Designing a Project (page 25); Embroider, Embellish, and Explore (page 78); Embroidery and Embellishment Stitch Reference Guide (page 114); and The Basics (page 152).

Color Discipline: Mono y Mono

Choose one color family for your fabrics from any number of solid, batik, or printed fabrics, ranging from light to dark (including white or black). Choose the embroidery and embellishments in the same value, in a lighter or darker value, or in any combination. You can also choose an additional accent color component.

Purple Haze, 10" × 10"

Shades of Gray, 7¾" × 7¾"

In this example I worked with the violet color family. I chose six cotton prints—two each in light, medium, and dark. For the crazy-pieced embroidery, I used perle cotton #8 in a light tone for the border row stitches, which are all worked in variations of the blanket stitch. I chose cotton floss in a medium tone, which is all worked in variations of the lazy daisy stitch. I used size 11 seed beads in a dark tone for the detail stitches and to create the border next to the binding.

This is a perfect example of a simple "penny rug," with appliquéd circles stacked on top of each other ranging in size from 2½" to 1½" to 1⅛". In an appliqué background, each component should stand out. In this example I worked from black to gray, with a high contrast between each color. The largest circle was layered with the medium and then the smaller circle. The embroidery began with the smaller circle, moving to the medium circle. The largest circle was then backed with another large circle. I used buttons to join the finished circles.

Crème de la Crème

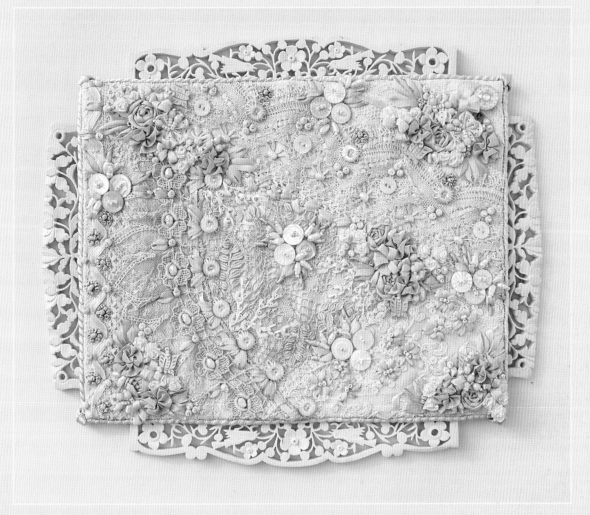

FINISHED SIZE: 9″ × 10¾″

For this example I chose to use shades of white, pearl, cream, rose beige, and dark beige. The background fabric is a doupioni silk in a cream color, with the vintage lace fabrics, collars, and trims appliquéd in a crazy-pieced pattern. I hand stitched the lace in place first. Then I stitched satin ribbon in sections to cover any raw edge of the lace or to create a design detail.

KEY ELEMENTS

Fabrics: silk fabric with lace fabric, lace collar, lace cuff, lengths of lace trim and satin ribbon

Construction: crazy-pieced appliqué

Embroidery design: vignette designs (page 105)

Embroidery and embellishment materials: 2 mm, 4 mm, and 7 mm silk embroidery ribbons; DMC perle cotton #12; ¼" rayon ribbon; vintage ⅜" mother-of-pearl buttons; 15 mm mother-of-pearl butterfly charms; freshwater pearls; and size 4 mm, 6 mm, 11 mm, and 15 mm Czech beads

EMBROIDERY STITCHES

Border row stitches: couched stitch, feather stitch, ribbon trim

Large components: woven rose stitch, old rose, rosette, embroidered buttons: lazy daisy stitch

Medium components: pointed petal stitch, silk ribbon flower stitch, accordion rose stitch, straight stitch flower

Small components: lazy daisy stitch, lazy daisy bullion tip stitch, French knot stitch flower, single bead stitch

Detail stitches: 3-wrap French knot stitch, single bead stitch, stacked bead stitch, beaded stamen stitch, stitched charms

Outer edge: couched rayon cord

FABRICS, EMBROIDERY, AND EMBELLISHMENT CHART

	Cream 1	Pearl 2		
Fabrics and lace				
Border row stitches	Pearl 2, ⅛" satin ribbon	White 5, 2 mm silk embroidery ribbon		
Large components	Rose beige 4, 7 mm silk embroidery ribbon	Dark beige 3, ¼" rayon ribbon	Pearl 2, ⅜" button	Cream 1, lace trim
Medium components	Cream 2, 4 mm silk embroidery ribbon	Rose beige 4, 4 mm silk embroidery ribbon	Pearl 2, 7 mm silk embroidery ribbon	
Small components	Pearl 2, 4 mm silk embroidery ribbon	Rose beige 4, 4 mm silk embroidery ribbon	Cream 1, 4 mm silk embroidery ribbon	Pearl 2, perle cotton #12
Detail stitches	Cream 1, size 6 seed beads	Cream 1, size 11 seed beads	White 5, size 15 seed beads	Cream 1, 4 mm Czech bead

Detail stitches (continued): Pearl 2, fresh-water pearls | Cream 1, mother-of-pearl charm

Color Discipline: Double Down

Choose two color families for your fabrics from any number of solid, batik, or printed fabrics. Choose the embroidery and embellishments in the same values, in lighter or darker values, or in any combination. You can also choose an additional accent color component.

Rustic Door, 13″ × 11⅝″

Log Cabin Heart Etui and Pincushion, etui 5″ × 4″, pincushion 2½″ × 3½″

This project started with two colors of cotton fabric, pieced in a modified log cabin design. Both the heart shape of the etui and the strip piecing for the pincushion lent themselves to the technique. For the embroidery threads I chose two fabric colors and added two more complementary colors. The perle cotton was in a darker tone of the fabric and the floss in a lighter tone.

For this piece, I chose batik fabrics that varied from rust to brown, plus one fabric in shades of midnight blue. I strip pieced the bottom portion of the base, crazy pieced the arch, and appliquéd the door into the center of the base. I added ribbons for a design element, both in the main body and as a border. The embroidery stitches were worked in two sizes of variegated perle cottons—#5 rust and #12 indigo blue. I used one stitch family for the border row stitches and another for the detail stitches. Blue celluloid buttons, brass buttons, and antiqued bronze charms completed the theme.

Bouncing Button Balloons

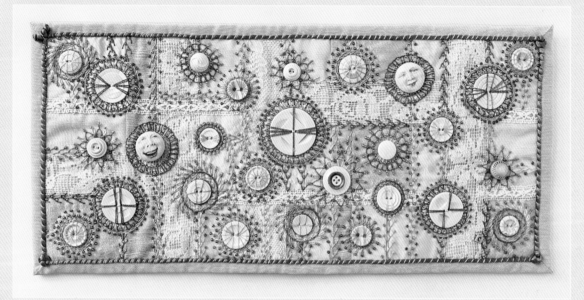

FINISHED SIZE: 7⅝" × 16¼"

I randomly strip pieced scraps of silk, moiré, and bengaline fabrics ranging from dusty sand to a golden yellow color. I included lace trim for additional design elements. I then stitched the vintage celluloid and fabric buttons at key points and sections. The subtle colors of the variegated threads were added to the almost monochromatic base. I chose to use Golden Grains Wildflowers thread, which had all the same colors as my background, lace, and buttons. I then added two more Wildflowers threads for accent colors: Coral Blush, ranging from light to dark coral, and Redwood, ranging from medium coral to dark rust. Rayon cord was couched around the fabric frame.

KEY ELEMENTS

Fabrics: silk, moiré, and bengaline fabrics; vintage lace trim; rayon cord

Construction: strip pieced

Embroidery design: straight-seam embroidery (page 79) and shadow embroidery (page 97)

Embroidery and embellishment materials: vintage celluloid buttons ranging in size from ½″ to 1¼, in cream; cloth buttons; Wildflowers thread; perle cotton #12; size 11 seed beads

EMBROIDERY STITCHES

Large component: stitched buttons fancy

Border row stitches: blanket stitch, feather stitch, chain stitch, feather stitch closed, chain stitch open, outline stitch

Decorative stitches: lazy daisy stitch, fly stitch

Detail stitches: French knot stitch, single bead stitch, grouped bead stitch

Outer edge: couched rayon cord

FABRICS, EMBROIDERY, AND EMBELLISHMENT CHART

	Golden Sand 1	Dusty Sand 2	Dusty Sand 2	Cream 3
Fabrics, laces, and buttons				
Button detail stitch	Golden Grains 4, perle cotton #12	Coral Blush 5, perle cotton #12	Redwood 6, perle cotton #12	
Border row stitches	Coral Blush 5, perle cotton #12	Redwood 6, perle cotton #12	Golden Grains 4, perle cotton #12	
Decorative stitches	Golden Grains 4, perle cotton #12	Coral Blush 5, perle cotton #12	Redwood 6, perle cotton #12	
Detail stitches	Coral Blush 5, perle cotton #12	Redwood 6, perle cotton #12	Golden Grains 4, perle cotton #12	
	Redwood 6, size 11 seed bead	Golden Grains 4, size 11 seed bead	Coral Blush 5, size 11 seed bead	
Couched cord frame	Redwood 6, rayon cord		Coral Blush 5, perle cotton #12	

Color Discipline: Triple Delight

Choose three color families for your fabrics from any number of solid, batik, or printed fabrics. Choose the embroidery and embellishments in the same values, in lighter or darker values, or in any combination. You can also choose an additional accent color component.

Rasta Pincushion with ceramic thimble, 3½" × 2½"

Serendipity, 6¼" × 6⅝"

The idea for the colors in the pincushion came from the ceramic thimble, a gift from my father-in-law. I chose solid-colored fabrics in yellow, green, and red for the pieced design. I found ombré cotton floss in the same colors as the fabrics and added black as an accent color. The border row stitches straddle each seam, and the decorative stitches were worked in a different color of thread on each side of the seam. I added black French knots as an accent to make the stitched design stand out.

This project started with two batik fabrics—one shaded from light to medium green, and the other in colors of green, plum, and rose. The embroidery was worked down each side of the seams in solid and hand-dyed colors to match and complement the two fabrics.

Batik Galaxy

FINISHED SIZE: 13¾" × 14¾"

*This project started with a group of batik fabrics in dark mustard, teal, and cranberry/
rust. The cranberry/rust fabric reminded me of the red ring around Mars, so I created a
galaxy in the center of the piece with wholecloth reverse appliqué. The copper and antiqued
brass finishes of the celestial-themed charms added an extra color element.*

KEY ELEMENTS

Fabrics: cotton batik fabrics

Construction: reverse appliqué and strip piecing

Embroidery design: straight-seam embroidery (page 78), appliqué embroidery (page 89), overall design (page 109)

Embroidery and embellishment materials: Anchor perle cotton #5 and DMC perle cotton #8, Valdani perle cotton #12, Wildflowers thread perle cotton #12, DMC cotton floss, ribbon thread, size 11 seed beads, copper and antiqued brass charms

EMBROIDERY STITCHES

Border row stitches: cretan stitch, feather stitch, blanket stitch closed, coral stitch, fern stitch modern, herringbone stitch, blanket stitch cobweb, blanket stitch, chain stitch, straight stitch

Decorative stitches: fly stitch, chain stitch, fly and loop stitch, fly stitch knotted, lazy daisy bullion tip stitch, lazy daisy stitch flower, buttonhole circle stitch

Detail stitches: 3-wrap French knot stitch, whip-stitch star, Celtic knot stitch, single bead stitch, grouped bead stitch, beaded charms, stitched buttons

FABRIC, EMBROIDERY, AND EMBELLISHMENT CHART

	Dark Mustard 1	Teal 2	Rusted Cranberry 3	Light Mustard 4	
Fabric	(fabric swatch)	(fabric swatch)	(fabric swatch)	(fabric swatch)	
Border row stitches	Teal 2, perle cotton #12	Rusted Cranberry 3, perle cotton #12	Dark Mustard 1, perle cotton #8	Teal 2, ribbon thread	Teal 2, perle cotton #5
Decorative stitches	Rusted Cranberry 3, 3 strands cotton floss	Light Mustard 4, 3 strands cotton floss	Teal 2, 3 strands cotton floss	Rusted Cranberry 3, 3 strands cotton floss	Teal 2, 3 strands cotton floss

Detail stitches	Teal 2, 3 strands cotton floss	Light Mustard 4, 3 strands cotton floss	Teal 2, 3 strands cotton floss	Rusted Cranberry 3, 3 strands cotton floss	Light Mustard 4, 3 strands cotton floss	Dark Mustard 1, perle cotton #8	Light Mustard 4, 3 strands cotton floss

Teal 2, size 11 seed beads	Rusted Cranberry 3, size 11 seed beads	Dark Mustard 1, size 11 seed beads	Charms
(seed beads)	(seed beads)	(seed beads)	(charms)

Color Discipline: Four Square

Choose four color families for your fabrics from any number of solid, batik, or printed fabrics. Choose the embroidery and embellishments in the same values, in lighter or darker values, or in any combination. You can also choose an additional accent color component.

Blue Lilies, 11¾″ × 11¾″

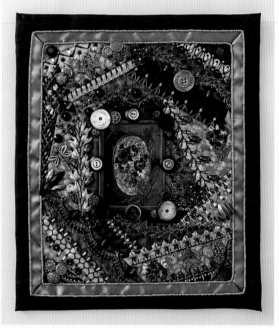

Midnight in Paris, 13″ × 11″

I combined three colors of silk and moiré with hand-dyed rayon lace and rayon appliqués. I chose to add plum for an accent color with lace and silk satin ribbons. The blue, teal, and green fabrics, threads, and silk embroidery ribbons are light and medium tones. I chose the plum threads in a light tone and the ribbon and lace in a dark tone. The glass buttons and large beads are light or medium tones; the size 11 seed beads are a dark tone.

The inspiration for this piece came from a bit of vintage lace and silk fabric that I hand dyed. I combined the silk and lace with cotton prints and solid fabrics in plum and gray. I chose ombré and satin ribbon for the flowers and ribbon trim. The vintage frame, charms, buttons, and beads provide charcoal and silver accents.

My Crazy Valentine

FINISHED SIZE: 9½" × 7¾"

This piece started with a greeting card from my mother. She embroidered the center heart section with luscious tones of red, green, and pink silk ribbon on a cream-colored background. I added two colors of green silk for the crazy piecing. I hand stitched vintage lace to frame the center and added additional pieces to the outer sections of crazy piecing. I then stitched ribbonwork rosettes into vignettes, with focal points created from buttons and larger glass flowers and leaves. The embroidery was stitched with silk embroidery ribbon, perle cotton, and cotton floss.

KEY ELEMENTS

Fabrics: moiré and silk fabrics, vintage lace, rayon cord

Construction: crazy pieced

Embroidery design: crazy-pieced embroidery (page 83), bordered designs (page 101), vignette designs (page 105)

Embroidery and embellishment materials: 2 mm, 4 mm, and 7 mm silk embroidery ribbon; Finca variegated perle cotton #8; Wildflowers and variegated DMC perle cotton #12; 12 mm flower rondelle; 8 mm flower button; glass leaves; metal charms; mother-of-pearl buttons; size 11 seed beads

EMBROIDERY STITCHES

Large components: rosette, stacked bead stitch

Medium components: pointed petal stitch, lazy daisy knot tip stitch, lazy daisy stitch

Detail components: accordion rose stitch, 3-wrap French knot stitch

Border row stitches: couched stitch, fern stitch modern

Decorative stitches: ribbon stitch

Detail stitches: 2-wrap French knot stitch, stitched charms, stitched buttons, bead combination stitch

Outer edge: couched rayon cord

FABRIC, EMBROIDERY, AND EMBELLISHMENT CHART

	Cream 1		Green 2		Cream 1	
Fabrics and lace						
Large components	Red 3A, 7 mm silk embroidery ribbon	Red 3C, ¼" ombré ribbon	Red 3C, ¼" ombré ribbon	Pink 4B, ¼" ombré ribbon	Flower and leaf	
Medium components	Green 2, 7 mm silk embroidery ribbon	Green 2, 7 mm silk embroidery ribbon	Green 2, 4 mm silk embroidery ribbon	Mother-of-pearl button		
Detail stitches	Pink 4, 4 mm silk embroidery ribbon	Pink 4, 4 mm silk embroidery ribbon	Pink 4, 4 mm silk embroidery ribbon	Red 3, 4 mm silk embroidery ribbon	Red 3, 4 mm silk embroidery ribbon	Glass flower button — Cream 1, perle cotton #8
Border row stitches	Green 2, 2 mm silk embroidery ribbon and perle cotton #12		Green 2, perle cotton #12			
Decorative stitches	Pink 4, 4 mm silk embroidery ribbon					
Detail stitches	Red 3, perle cotton #8	Pink 4, perle cotton #12				
Couched cord frame	Green 2, rayon cord	Green 2, perle cotton #12				

Color Discipline: Five and Dime

Choose five color families for your fabrics from any number of solid, batik, or printed fabrics. Choose the embroidery and embellishments in the same values, in lighter or darker values, or in any combination. You can also choose an additional accent color component.

Jelly Beans, 8¾" × 8¾"

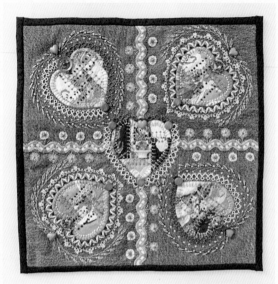

Country Hearts, 14" × 14"

This project began with a felt square with a fabulous floral pattern. I chose four additional felt squares in solid colors to complete the palette. The circles were reverse appliquéd, working from large to small. Soutache trim, hand stitched around the appliqué shapes, created additional design elements. Seed and large beads, buttons, and sequins were chosen in the five colors of the palette. This piece was entirely embroidered and embellished with beads.

This project started with a few pieced appliqués made from leftover fabrics from *50s Flashback* (next page). The base was made from four squares cut from a pair of old jeans, with vintage rickrack trim covering the raw edges of the seams. I chose five colors from the prints and used perle cotton #8 in both light and medium tones for a total of ten colors. The large rickrack trim was embellished with ribbonwork rosettes made from picot-edge ombré ribbon with glass bead centers.

50s Flashback

FINISHED SIZE: 12¼″ × 12¼″

This project truly embraces generations of treasured bits of stash. I started with a vintage floral fabric that had been a birdcage cover (most likely from the 1950s). I then found four floral fabrics from both my mom's stash and mine and added beige as an accent to make it five colors for the palette. I added some vintage ribbons, tatted trim, and celluloid buttons from the 1940s. The embroidery was worked with perle cotton and cotton floss and embellished with ribbonwork flowers, buttons, charms, and beads.

KEY ELEMENTS

Fabrics: cotton fabrics; tatted lace; rayon cord; jacquard, satin, and grosgrain ribbons; lace appliqué

Construction: crazy pieced

Embroidery design: crazy-pieced embroidery (page 83)

Embroidery and embellishment materials: Finca and Anchor perle cotton #8, Finca and DMC cotton floss, vintage and new rickrack trim, vintage buttons, glass flower-shaped buttons and beads, size 11 seed beads, brass charms

EMBROIDERY STITCHES

Border row stitches: feather stitch double, chain stitch feathered, blanket stitch, fly stitch, feather stitch, chain stitch open, feather stitch closed, fly stitch crossed, outline stitch, ribbon trim, rickrack trim, lace trim

Decorative stitches: bell flower stitch, lazy daisy stitch, looped tendril stitch, lazy daisy bullion tip stitch, fly stitch side by side, lazy daisy knot tip stitch

Detail stitches: 3-wrap French knot stitch, pistil stitch, stacked bead stitch, stem and flower stitch, stitched charms, picot tip stitch

Large components: rosette, stitched buttons, embroidered buttons: French knot stitch, button spider, stacked buttons, clustered buttons

Outer edge: couched rayon cord

FABRIC, EMBROIDERY, AND EMBELLISHMENT CHART

	50s Blue 1	Blue 1	Coral 2	Green 3	Yellow 4	Yellow 4
Fabric						
	Coral 2, ribbon	Coral 2, rickrack	Green 3, satin ribbon	Yellow 3, satin ribbon	Blue 1, tatted lace	Beige 5, polka dot
Ribbon trim						

FABRIC, EMBROIDERY, AND EMBELLISHMENT CHART *continued*

Border row stitches	Green 3, perle cotton #8	Green 3, perle cotton #8	Blue and cream 1, tatted lace	Beige 6, perle cotton #8	Beige 5, perle cotton #8	Coral 2, perle cotton #8		
Decorative stitches	Blue 1, cotton floss	Yellow 4, cotton floss	Yellow 4, perle cotton	Coral 2, cotton floss	Blue 1, cotton floss	Green 3, cotton floss	Green 3, cotton floss	
Detail stitches	Coral 2, cotton floss	Brass charms	Blue 1, cotton floss	Vintage buttons	Brass charms	Beige 6, cotton floss		
Vignettes	Beige 6, grosgrain ribbon	Yellow 5, checkered ribbon	Blue 1, rickrack	Vintage buttons	Flower buttons and beads			
Detail stitches	Blue 1, 4 mm silk embroidery ribbon	Coral 2, cotton floss	Green 3, cotton floss	Yellow 4, perle cotton	Coral 2, silk embroidery ribbon	Green 3, silk embroidery ribbon	Green 3, perle cotton #8	Green 3, size 15 seed bead	Yellow 4, size 11 seed bead
Framed ribbon borders	Green 3, Yellow 4	Beige 5, rayon cord	Blue 1, rickrack	Coral 2, flower trim				

Color Discipline: Colors and More Colors

Choose six or more color families for your fabrics from any number of solid, batik, or printed fabrics. Choose the embroidery and embellishments in the same values, in lighter or darker values, or in any combination. You can also choose an additional accent color component.

Flower Child, 5¾" × 6½"

This little square started with several hand-dyed components—a silk jacquard fabric and three silk embroidery ribbons, each dyed with two complementary colors. In addition I used solid silk embroidery ribbons and variegated cotton floss.

Victoriana, side 1, 9¼" × 9¼"

Solid colors of silk and rayon fabrics complement the rayon floral print. Additional colors create the deep, rich tones associated with the Victorian era. The embroidered design was worked off the seams and within the strips of fabric. The embroidery materials are in lighter and darker tones than the fabrics. Vintage glass buttons from the Victorian era, as well as newer glass buttons and charms, help create the theme.

Merrily We Go Around

FINISHED SIZE: 6¾" × 7¾"

I took a square of linen fabric in a solid color and gathered threads in many colors. The background was machine stitched with variegated cotton sewing thread in the image of a free-form spiral, creating a bordered design for the floral-themed embroidery stitches to follow. The five flower designs with a stalk and leaf, two vine designs, and one small flower were all worked in seventeen colors of cotton floss. These eight components were repeated throughout the spiral.

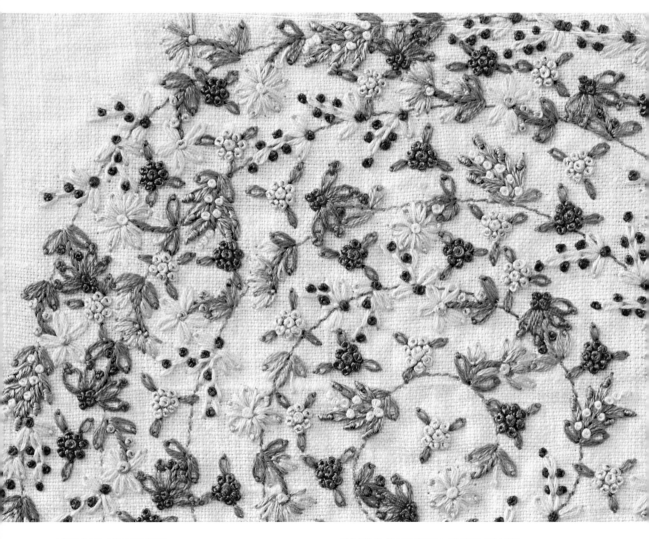

KEY ELEMENTS

Fabrics: linen and cotton fabrics

Construction: whole cloth

Embroidery design: bordered designs (page 101)

Embroidery and embellishment materials: 12-weight sewing thread and cotton floss

EMBROIDERY STITCHES

Stalks: outline stitch, lazy daisy stitch

Flowers: lazy daisy stitch flower (3, 4, 5, and 6 petals) using the lazy daisy stitch and lazy daisy bullion tip stitch

Detail stitches: 3-wrap French knot stitch, straight stitch, fly stitch

Small flowers: French knot stitch flower, lazy daisy stitch

Vines: feather stitch, chain stitch, lazy daisy stitch

Details: 3-wrap French knot stitch

FABRIC, EMBROIDERY, AND EMBELLISHMENT CHART

Fabric	Linen 1	Green 2A, 12-weight sewing thread			
Stalk	Green 2B, cotton floss	Green 2C, cotton floss			
Flower	Pink/yellow 3A, cotton floss	Violet/pink 3B, cotton floss	Blue/shell 3C, cotton floss	Rose/grape 3D, cotton floss	Yellow/lavender 3E, cotton floss
Small flower with leaves	Medium purple 4A, cotton floss	Dark purple 4B, cotton floss	Green 2D, cotton floss		
Vine with details	Green 2E, cotton floss	Light purple 4C, cotton floss			

Color Discipline: Piggyback Jack

Start with a variegated thread or ribbon; then choose color families for the fabrics, embroidery, and embellishments in the same values, in lighter or darker values, or in any combination. You can also choose an additional accent color component.

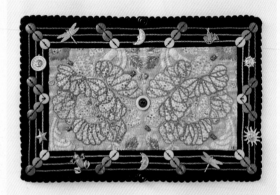

Santa Fe Summer, 9½″ × 14½″

The maize-colored cotton print bordered in black linen creates a bold design. The large abstract flowers in the print provide room for the embroidery stitches. I combined a variegated colorway of cotton floss with solid-colored floss in mustard, coral, and turquoise. Three rows of chain stitches were worked in each of the solid-colored borders of the design, with buttons and charms used for details. I hand stitched braid to the outer edges.

California Dreamin', 11¼″ × 11¼″

This project started with a variegated thread and two pieces of marbleized fabrics that provided a variety of colors to work with. I chose six color families: pink, purple, turquoise, yellow, peach, and green. Perle cotton #5 and cotton floss in variegated, ombré, and solid colors were used for the embroidery stitches.

Umbria

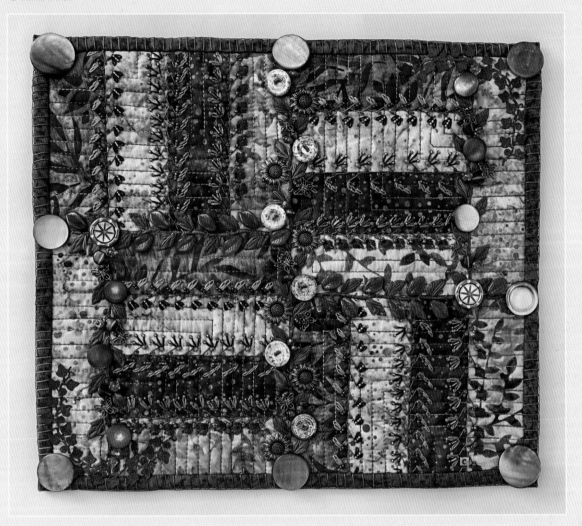

FINISHED SIZE: 11¼" × 12⅞"

This project started with four printed batik fabrics in rich browns, rust, and cranberry colors. I found variegated perle cotton that picked up all of those colors. I then chose the remainder of the embroidery and embellishments to match the thread. I strip pieced four sections with the four fabrics and then stitched these into a larger base. I added a leaf trim in the center and in the outer sections of two sections. I stitched vintage shell buttons, copper charms, and glass buttons around the leaf trim and added metal trim to two of the corners. The binding was embroidered with a blanket stitch and vintage buttons.

KEY ELEMENTS

Fabrics: cotton printed batik fabrics, leaf trim

Construction: strip pieced

Embroidery design: straight-seam embroidery (page 79) and embroidered trims (page 93)

Embroidery and embellishment materials: machine quilted with 12-weight cotton thread, variegated perle cotton #8, cotton floss, size 11 and 15 seed beads, size 11 Delica beads, bugle beads, 3 mm and 8 mm Czech beads, vintage carved mother-of-pearl and dyed mussel shell buttons, glass buttons, copper-plated charms

KEY ELEMENTS

Border row stitches: feather stitch, leaf trim

Decorative stitches: fly stitch, lazy daisy stitch, lazy daisy knot tip stitch, chain stitch, fly stitch side by side, looped tendril stitch

Detail stitches: single bead stitch, grouped bead stitch, stacked bead stitch, bead cascade stitch, stitched buttons, stitched charms, beaded buttons

Outer edge: blanket stitch

FABRIC, EMBROIDERY, AND EMBELLISHMENT CHART

	Driftwood 1	Nutmeg 2	Dusty Rose 3	Cabernet 4			
Fabric							
Vine, quilting thread, and border row stitches	Copper 6, vine		Variegated 5, 12-weight sewing thread	Variegated 5, perle cotton #8			
Decorative stitches	Nutmeg 2, cotton floss	Driftwood 1, cotton floss	Cabernet 4, cotton floss	Dusty Rose 3, cotton floss			
Detail stitches	Matte Rose 3, size 11 seed bead	Matte Copper 6, size 11 Delica bead	Matte Nutmeg 2, size 11 seed bead	Copper 6, bugle bead	Driftwood 1, size 11 seed bead	Driftwood 1, 3 mm Czech bead	Matte Cabernet 4, size 11 seed bead
Additional details	Vintage buttons		Copper 6, sunflower and butterfly charm	Nutmeg 2, glass leaf	Driftwood 1, flower button	Driftwood 1, 8 mm Czech bead	Nutmeg 2, size 15 seed bead

Color Discipline: Follow the Leader

Choose any number of color families for your fabrics, threads, ribbons, and embellishments. Choose one color of thread to use for the border row stitches to create a strong design element and pull in the additional components. Choose the remaining embroidery and embellishments in the same colors of the fabric or in lighter or darker colors. You can also choose an additional accent color component.

Harlequin Peacock, 9¼" × 7½"

Melted Crayons, 15⅜" × 15⅜"

Four solid colors of silk were strip pieced together to create the base for this purse. The fabric base was machine quilted with Sulky metallic thread. Vintage gold lace was hand stitched to one edge of a seam; gold trim was hand stitched in a curved design that straddled a seam or ran along the center of a strip of fabric. Metallic and rayon threads, seed beads, bugle beads, and vintage sequins were used for the embroidery and embellishment design.

Tiny bits of precious silk fabrics were crazy pieced into squares and a strip-pieced border. This wild display of color was bordered with black silk fabric and satin ribbon. The border rows were worked in black buttonhole twist, with the detail stitches worked in variegated perle cotton. Button details were stitched down with perle cotton and rayon floss.

Lady Bird's Bzzy Garden

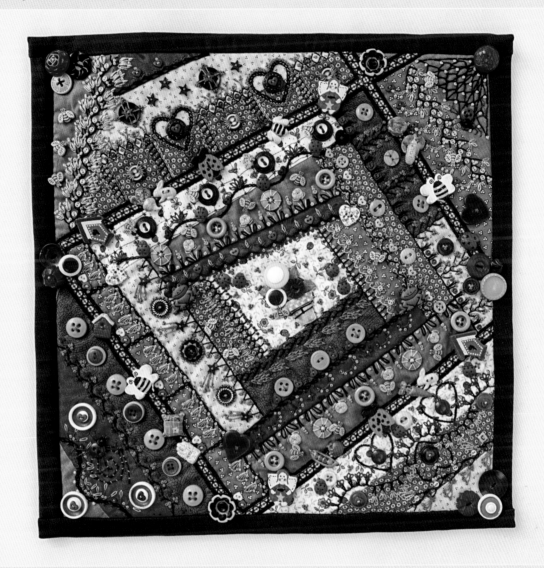

FINISHED SIZE: 14″ × 13¾″

I combined two prints that had darling little ladybugs with solid and printed cotton fabrics. The cotton prints all had one color in common—black, which became a design detail and was used to outline each strip of fabric with the border row stitches. The decorative and detail stitches were worked in the same colors of the fabric. The quaint vintage and new buttons provided the theme.

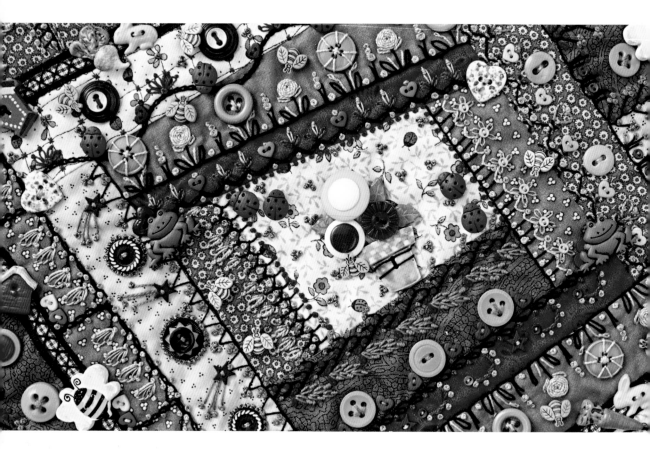

KEY ELEMENTS

Fabrics: solid and printed cotton fabrics, checkered and grosgrain ribbons

Construction: crazy pieced

Embroidery design: crazy-pieced embroidery (page 83)

Embroidery and embellishment materials: perle cotton #8 and #10; novelty, vintage celluloid, and new plastic buttons

EMBROIDERY STITCHES

Border row stitches: blanket stitch, feather stitch double, cretan stitch, chain stitch zigzag, loop stitch leaves and stalk, herringbone stitch detailed, chain stitch double, blanket stitch closed, blanket stitch up and down, feather and chain stitch single, feather stitch random, cross stitch row, chain stitch cable, feather and chain stitch, ribbon trim

Decorative stitches: fly stitch, lazy daisy stitch flower, lazy daisy bullion tip stitch, woven rose stitch, chain stitch loop, heart stitch, looped tendril stitch, fly stitch knotted, lazy daisy stitch, chain stitch open, outline stitch, lacy web stitch, knobby cobbleweb stitch

Detail stitches: 1-wrap, 2-wrap, and 3-wrap French knot stitch; stamen stitch; stitched buttons; stitched buttons fancy; stacked buttons; embroidered buttons; clustered buttons; button spider

FABRIC, EMBROIDERY, AND EMBELLISHMENT CHART

Border fabric and ribbons	Black 8, border fabric	Black 8, grosgrain ribbon	Cranberry 2, checkered ribbon	Novelty buttons			

Fabric	Mustard 1, ladybug	Cranberry 2	Brown 3	Green 4	Rose 5	Chamois 6	Blue 7

Border row stitches	Black 8, perle cotton #8						

Decorative stitches	Cranberry 2, perle cotton #8	Brown 3, perle cotton #8	Green 4, perle cotton #10	Rose 5, perle cotton #8	Chamois 6, perle cotton #8	Blue 7, perle cotton #8	Mustard 1, perle cotton #8

Detail stitches	Brown 3, perle cotton #8	Green 4, perle cotton #10	Rose 5, perle cotton #8	Chamois 6, perle cotton #8	Blue 7, perle cotton #8	Mustard 1, perle cotton #8	Cranberry 2, perle cotton #8

Button details	Cranberry 2	Brown 3	Green 4	Rose 5	Chamois 6	Blue 7	Mustard 1

EMBROIDER, EMBELLISH, AND EXPLORE

Embroidery as a Seam Treatment: Straight-Seam Embroidery, page 79

Embroidery as a Seam Treatment: Crazy-Pieced Embroidery, page 83

Embroidery as a Seam Treatment: Appliqué Embroidery, page 89

Embroidery as a Seam Treatment: Embroidered Trims, page 93

Embroidery as a Design Element: Shadow Embroidery, page 97

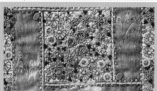

Embroidery as a Design Element: Bordered Designs, page 101

Embroidery as a Design Element: Vignette Designs, page 105

Embroidery as a Design Element: Overall Design, page 109

Embroidery Applications

The embroidery stitches included in the embroidery and embellishment stitch reference guide (page 114) can be worked following a seam, following a shape or an imaginary line, or to fill in an entire area or space. In most cases, the pieced fabric base and overall design of the project will dictate the embroidery application that you will use.

EMBROIDERY AS A SEAM TREATMENT

Seam treatments are described as embroidered stitches that follow a stitched seam of fabric, edge of lace, or edge of ribbon. A seam treatment begins with a border row stitch. This row of stitches can then be embellished with decorative and detail stitches, a composite stitch, or a combination of stitches.

EMBROIDERY AS A DESIGN ELEMENT

Embroidery can also be used as an overall design element, which differs from the decoration of a seam. The design can mirror or shadow a shape, fill in entire sections of fabric, work small designs into open spaces, or fill the entire base of a fabric.

Straight-Seam Embroidery

Strip-pieced sections, nine-patch squares, and Log Cabin blocks all have straight seams that can be embroidered and embellished. Straight-seam embroidery is worked off of an existing seam in the pieced base. The border row of embroidery can be worked on either side of the seam, or it can straddle the seam. If the border row straddles a seam, each side can be embroidered with the same or a different group of decorative and detail stitches.

Blue Heart Etui, 5" × 4"

This etui was pieced in a modified log cabin design using three different cotton prints. All the border row stitches were worked in green perle cotton. Cotton floss in green, blue, pink, rose, and yellow were used for the decorative and detail stitches. The vintage

glass button sewn to the top section repeats the lazy daisy flower design.

Rasta Pincushion, 3½" × 2½"

The embroidery design becomes a strong element when using solid-color fabrics and a simple pieced design. I chose ombré cotton floss in the same colors as the yellow, green, and red fabrics. The border row stitches straddle each seam, and the decorative stitches were worked in a different color of thread on either side of the seam. Black was added as an accent color and was only worked in French knots to make the stitched design stand out.

Paris Flea Market, 14½" × 14½"

I pieced a nine-patch design using a charm packet from Moda Fabrics. The center squares were divided into four sections—two aqua and two peach. The outer border used the remaining squares in the packet. Each center square in the same color was worked with the same group of stitches. Opposite squares of the border row were worked in the same group of stitches. All the embroidery was stitched in perle cotton #8. The border row stitches were worked in one color, the decorative stitches in a second color, and the detail stitches in a third color. Vintage mother-of-pearl buttons were stitched around the border, and additional buttons were stitched in the center and corners.

Charmed Square

FINISHED SIZE: 8″ × 8″

This small square was pieced with a few leftover squares from a Moda charm pack. I added two complementary fabrics to complete the nine-patch design and border. The border row stitches were worked in one color of perle cotton #8 to straddle each seam. The decorative and detail stitches were worked in five colors of cotton floss and two colors of size 11 seed beads. The color and stitch changed depending on which side of the border row they were stitched. I used three colors of glass buttons and charms and added brass buttons as an accent color.

KEY ELEMENTS

Fabrics: cotton prints

Construction: nine-patch assembly

Color discipline: Follow the Leader (page 74)

Embroidery and embellishment materials: Anchor perle cotton #8, DMC cotton floss, size 11 seed beads, glass and button charms, vintage brass, celluloid buttons

COLOR CODE

Fabric: Rose 1, Olive 2, Brown 3

Perle cotton: Chamois 4a

3 strands of cotton floss: Rose 1b, Brown 3b, Chamois 4b, Garnet 5b, Pine 6b

Size 11 seed beads: Olive 2c, Garnet 5c

Larger glass beads and buttons: Olive 2d leaf, Garnet 5d flower button, Mustard 7d flower button

Buttons: Garnet 5e plastic heart button, Brass 8e button, Multicolor 9e celluloid button

EMBROIDERY STITCH AND COLOR DIAGRAM

Fabric	Border row stitch/color	Decorative stitch/color	Decorative stitch/color	Detail stitch/color		Detail stitch/color		
Rose 1, center	Blanket stitch	Lazy daisy stitch	Fly stitch	3-wrap French knot stitch		Beaded buttons		Stitched buttons
	Chamois 4a	Garnet 5b	Pine 6b	Chamois 4b		Garnet 5e	Olive 2c	Multicolor 9e
Olive 2	Feather stitch (side 1)	Lazy daisy stitch flower	Fly stitch	3-wrap French knot stitch	Single bead stitch	Stitched buttons		
	Chamois 4a	Rose 1b	Brown 3b	Chamois 4b	Garnet 5c	Brass 8e		
Rose 1	Feather stitch (side 2)	Looped tendril stitch	Lazy daisy stitch	3-wrap French knot stitch	Single bead stitch	Beaded charms		
	Chamois 4a	Garnet 5b	Pine 6b	Chamois 4b	Olive 2c	Olive 2d		Garnet 5c
Brown 3	Herringbone stitch	Straight stitch detail	3-wrap French knot stitch	3-wrap French knot stitch		Beaded buttons		
	Chamois 4a	Garnet 5b	Brown 3b	Pine 6b		Garnet 5d		Mustard 7d

Crazy-Pieced Embroidery

Crazy-patched and crazy-pieced blocks have interesting lines, curves, and open sections that can be embroidered and embellished. The embroidery is very similar to straight-seam embroidery, though it has a tendency to be more elaborate. Additional decorative and detail stitches are often added to the border row stitches. The embroidery design can be worked over seams or can flow over several sections of fabric. In addition, vignettes are often worked into corner or middle sections of fabric.

Vintage celluloid buttons, new glass buttons, and charms were added for additional embellishments. This project was started several years ago, and I was finally able to finish it because I had created an embroider-by-number chart that I kept with the project.

Lady Bird 2, 14" × 13¾"

Crazy Gal, 8¼" × 6¾"

The base of this project was pieced with cotton prints, moiré, cotton velveteen, and wool blend fabrics. The embroidered design was stitched along the seams, over several seams, and in the center of the larger fabric shapes. The embroidery stitches were worked in perle cotton #5 and #8, cotton floss, and seed beads.

This crazy-pieced base has sections of lace and ribbon that create a frame around the center section. Strip-pieced borders frame the outer portion of the rectangle, and a wooden frame filled with flowers, garden tools, and buttons borders the top section. The embroidery is worked off the seams, over several seams, and in the center of the larger fabric shapes. Vignettes of ribbonwork flowers can be spotted throughout the design.

Midnight in Paris, 13″ × 11″

This wallhanging was crazy pieced with cotton solids, prints, silk, and vintage laces. The embroidery was worked in 4 mm and 7 mm silk embroidery ribbon, silk perle, perle cotton, and cotton floss. Vintage buttons, beads, an antique metal frame, and charms embellish the work. A ribbon border with bead details showcases the piecing and frames the project.

Crazy Lady

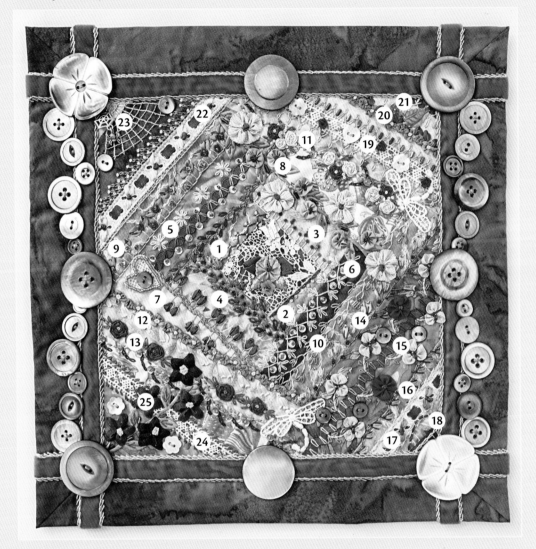

FINISHED SIZE: 12¾″ × 12¾″

Cotton prints, batik fabrics, and vintage lace edging were crazy pieced to create this square. The embroidery design straddles the seams and flows within large sections of fabric. Lace appliqués and ribbonwork flowers can be found in corner sections, within large sections of fabric, and on a trim that flows over several rows of fabric. Eight colors were chosen for the silk embroidery ribbons, threads, ribbons for the flowers, and other embellishments.

KEY ELEMENTS

Fabrics: cotton prints, vintage cotton lace, rayon appliqués

Construction: crazy piecing

Color discipline: Colors and More Colors (page 66)

Embroidery and embellishment materials: 4mm silk embroidery ribbon, perle cotton #8, silk perle #8, cotton floss, seed beads, charms, sequins, glass buttons, woven and silk bias ribbon, rayon hem tape, leaf trim, new and vintage rickrack trim, velvet ribbon, vintage shell buttons

COLOR CODE

Fabric: Rose 1, Light Brown 2, Medium Green 3, Butterfly Print Blue 4, Cranberry 5, Dark Brown 6, Light Green 7, Ecru 8

4mm silk embroidery ribbon: Rose 1a, Medium Green 3a, Blue 4a, Cranberry 5a, Dark Brown 6a, Ecru 8a

Perle cotton #8 or silk perle #8: Rose 1b, Light Brown 2b, Medium Green 3b, Blue 4b, Variegated Cranberry 5b, Dark Brown 6b, Light Green 7b, Ecru 8b

Cotton floss: Rose 1c, Medium Green 3c, Variegated Cranberry 5c

Metallic floss: Gold 9c

Seed beads: Rose 1d, Medium Green 3d, Cranberry 5d, Dark Green 7d, Gold 9d, Copper 10d

Large beads: Copper 10e bugle bead

Embellishments: Rose 11f sequin, Cranberry 5f flower button, Ecru 8f butterfly charm, Gold 9f leaf sequin, Dark Rose 11f glass flower, Mother-of-Pearl 12f button

Ribbon: Rose 1g grosgrain ribbon, Blue 4g silk bias ribbon, Cranberry 5g rayon hem tape, Ecru 8g rayon hem tape

Trim: Medium Light Brown 2h velvet ribbon, Medium Green 3h leaf trim, Cranberry 5h satin ribbon, Dark Brown 6h rickrack trim, Ecru 8h lace trim, Dark Green 10h rickrack trim, Dark Rose 11h ribbon trim

EMBROIDERY STITCH AND COLOR DIAGRAM

Fabric and row	Border row		Decorative stitches			Detail stitches	
Center: Dark Brown 6 and lace	Rosette		Picot tip stitch	Bead cascade stitch		Stacked bead stitch	
	Rose 1g		Rose 11f / Cranberry 5d	Ecru 8f / Gold 9d		Gold 9f / Gold 9d	
1. Rose 1	Herringbone stitch		Straight stitch details			2-wrap French knot stitch	
	Dark Brown 6b		Light Green 7b			Ecru 8b	
2. Rose 1	Chain stitch					2-wrap French knot stitch	
	Dark Brown 6b					Light Green 7b	
3. Light Green 7	Blanket stitch short-long-short					3-wrap French knot stitch	
	Ecru 8b					Variegated Cranberry 5c	
4. Medium Green 3	Feather stitch random		Lazy daisy stitch	Lazy daisy stitch		3-wrap French knot stitch	
	Blue 4b		Variegated Cranberry 5c	Medium Green 3c		Dark Brown 6b	
5. Light Brown 2	Embroidered trim	Lazy daisy stitch	Lazy daisy stitch flower	Single bead stitch		Stacked bead stitch	
	Dark Green 10h	Variegated Cranberry 5b	Ecru 8b	Rose 1d		Rose 1f	Dark Green 7d
6. Dark Brown 6	Herringbone stitch	Straight stitch details	Lazy daisy stitch	3-wrap French knot stitch		Stacked bead stitch	
	Light Green 7b	Rose 1b	Ecru 8b	Rose 1b		Rose 1f	Dark Green 7d
7. Ecru 8	Blanket stitch zipper row		Chain stitch	Lazy daisy stitch		Fly stitch	
	Rose 1b		Medium Green 3b	Dark Brown 6a		Medium Green 3b	
8. Butterfly Print Blue 4	Embroidered trim	Fly stitch	Rosette	3-wrap French knot stitch	Rosette	Single bead stitch	
	Medium Green 3h	Medium Green 3c	Rose 1g	Dark Brown 6a	Blue 4g	Copper 10e	
9. Rose 1	Blanket stitch grouped even		Lazy daisy stitch	Accordion rose stitch		Single bead stitch	
	Light Brown 2b		Medium Green 3a	Blue 4a / Cranberry 5a		Cranberry 5d	
10. Rose 1	Feather stitch		Lazy daisy stitch			3-wrap French knot stitch	
	Light Brown 2b		Light Green 7b			Blue 4b	
11. Medium Green 3	Couched stitch	Chain stitch	Woven rose stitch	Lazy daisy stitch		3-wrap French knot stitch	Stacked bead stitch
	Ecru 8b / Medium Green 3c	Dark Brown 6b	Cranberry 5a / Rose 1a / Ecru 8a	Medium Green 3c		Rose 1c	Rose 1f / Gold 9d
12. Light Green 7	Embroidered trim		Ribbon stitch			3-wrap French knot stitch	
	Dark Rose 11h		Rose 1a			Ecru 8b	

Fabric and row	Border row		Decorative stitches		Detail stitches		
13. Light Green 7	Couched stitch	Chain stitch	Woven rose stitch	Lazy daisy stitch	3-wrap French knot stitch	Stacked bead stitch	
	Ecru 8b	Dark Brown 6b	Cranberry 5a	Medium Green 3c	Variegated Cranberry 5c	Rose 1f	Gold 9d
14. Light Brown 2	Feather stitch		Ribbon stitch	Fly and straight stitches	3-wrap French knot stitch		
	Medium Green 3b		Blue 4a	Rose 1c	Dark Brown 6b		
15. Light Brown 2, center of strip	Embroidered trim	Lazy daisy stitch	Rosette	3-wrap French knot stitch	Rosette	Straight stitch	
	Dark Green 10h	Variegated Cranberry 5b	Cranberry 5g	Dark Brown 6a	Ecru 8g	Cranberry 5a	
	Outline stitch		Lazy daisy stitch		Stitched buttons		
	Ecru 8b		Light Green 7b		Mother-of-Pearl 12f		
16. Medium Green 3	Chain stitch		Lazy daisy stitch		Fly stitch		
	Blue 4b		Rose 1c		Dark Brown 6b		
17. Medium Green 3, center strip	Lace trim		Herringbone stitch	Lazy daisy stitch	3-wrap French knot stitch		
	Ecru 8h	Cranberry 5h	Rose 1b	Medium Green 3a	Dark Brown 6a		
18. Dark Brown 6	Couched stitch		Chain stitch		Blanket stitch		
	Dark Brown 6a		Light Green 7b		Ecru 8b		
19. Ecru 8	Lace trim	Cross stitch	Fly and loop stitch	Fly stitch	Stitched buttons	Single bead stitch	
	Ecru 8h	Blue 4b	Light Brown 2b	Rose 1b	Mother-of-Pearl 12f	Cranberry 5f	Copper 10e
20. Ecru 8, center of strip	Embroidered trim	3-wrap French knot stitch	Lazy daisy stitch	Picot tip stitch	Stitched charm		
	Dark Rose 11h	Ecru 8b	Dark Brown 6a	Dark Rose 11f / Cranberry 5d	Gold 9f	Gold 9d	
21. Dark Brown 6	Herringbone stitch		Lazy daisy stitch				
	Light Green 7b		Rose 1b				
22. Dark Brown 6	Embroidered trim	Blanket stitch	Lazy daisy stitch	Chain stitch	3-wrap French knot stitch	2-wrap French knot stitch	
	Ecru 8h / Cranberry 5h	Light Green 7b	Rose 1a	Blue 4b	Dark Brown 6a	Rose 1c	
23. Light Green 7	Outline stitch		Outline stitch		Stitched buttons		
	Ecru 8b		Gold 9c		Mother-of-Pearl 12f		
24. Light Brown 2	Embroidered trim		Cross stitch		Lazy daisy stitch		
	Ecru 8h		Blue 4b		Medium Green 3c		
25. Light Brown 2, center	Embroidered trim	Fly stitch	Rickrack flower	Accordion rose stitch	Single bead stitch	Stitched buttons	
	Medium Green 3h	Medium Green 3c	Dark Brown 6h	Rose 1a	Copper 10e	Mother-of-Pearl 12f	

Appliqué Embroidery

Appliqué embroidery, which is worked off the edge of an object, can also function as a stitch to attach the appliqué to the fabric base. The embroidered design can be worked into the appliqué shape or built off the shape's outer edge. This embroidery can be applied to straight, curved, or other shaped objects. The embroidery stitch can start anywhere around a circular shape; begin a straight shape at one corner edge. When working with a shape that is a mirror image, such as a heart, embroider one side first and then the other side, mirroring the direction and quantity of the stitches.

Labeled Purse, 9½″ × 8¾″

This purse was a fun exercise in finding a way to use all the manufacturer's labels that I had collected over the years. My friend Phred worked as a tailor for Barneys New York, and many of these labels came from his clients. The background fabric is silk; the embroidery threads are perle cotton #5, #8, and #12. The edges of the labels were embroidered with variations of the blanket, chain, cross, straight, and French knot stitches. Vintage buttons were sprinkled and stitched throughout the piece.

Fireworks, 8⅝" × 9⅛"

This project started with a printed felt fabric that was loaded with all kinds of colors. I used a black felt square for the base, and then reverse appliquéd circles with the printed felt. I also cut the center of each circle into a square shape and reverse appliquéd each square with black felt. I found variegated cotton floss in the same colors as the printed felt. I chose five additional solid colors of floss to complete the palette. The border row stitches use the variegated floss; the decorative and detail stitches use the solid-colored floss.

The Village Sleeps Tonight, 8¾" × 11¾"

Synthetic felt and precut rayon/wool blend felt were used to create this fun appliqué wallhanging with a hand-dyed rickrack trim border. I chose eight colors of felt components and used eight colors of perle cotton #8 in solid and variegated colorways. The embroidery stitches are in the same color as each component. I refer to this color choice as "deep impact," which can be applied to any of the color disciplines.

Country Hearts

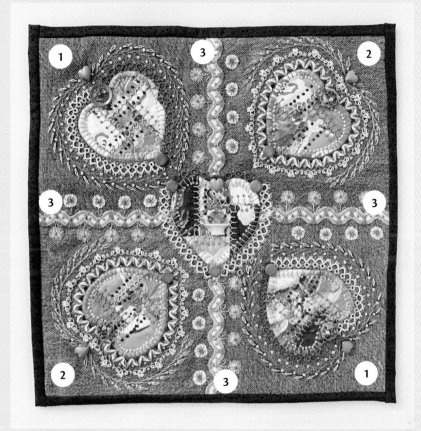

FINISHED SIZE: 14″ × 14″

The simple design for this wallhanging began with a few pieced appliqués that I made from leftover floral prints from 50s Flashback (page 63). I cut and pieced the denim background from a pair of old jeans. I found the vintage lace and rickrack trim at a thrift store, and the odd blue color matched one of the floral prints. I used the wider rickrack trims to hide the raw-edged seams of the denim squares. I chose five colors from the prints and used perle cotton #8 in both light and medium tones for a total of ten colors. All ten colors were worked into each heart appliqué; if I used a light color for one stitch, then I stitched the next one in a medium color and so on. Each appliqué was embellished with vintage tatting or rickrack trim and buttons. The large rickrack trim was embellished with ribbonwork rosettes made from picot-edge ombré ribbon.

KEY ELEMENTS

Fabrics: denim, cotton prints, vintage tatted lace, rickrack trim

Construction: appliqué

Color discipline: Five and Dime (page 62)

Embroidery and embellishment materials: perle cotton #8, picot-edge ombré ribbon, 4 mm glass beads, vintage celluloid buttons

COLOR CODE

Perle cotton #8: Light Pink 1, Medium Pink 2, Light Coral 3, Medium Coral 4, Light Yellow 5, Medium Yellow 6, Light Blue 7, Medium Blue 8, Light Green 9, Medium Green 10

Beads: Green 11

Ribbon: Yellow Ombré 12

EMBROIDERY STITCH AND COLOR HEART 1

Inner edge		Outer edge							Inside square			
Border row stitch/color	Detail stitch/color	Tatted lace/color		Border row stitch/color	Decorative stitch/color	Decorative stitch/color	Detail stitch/color	Border row stitch/color		Detail stitch/color	
Blanket stitch	3-wrap French knot stitch	3-wrap French knot stitch		Feather stitch	Lazy daisy stitch	Fly stitch	3-wrap French knot stitch	Cretan stitch		3-wrap French knot stitch	
Light Green 9	Medium Yellow 6	Light Blue 7	Medium Coral 4	Medium Green 10	Light Pink 1	Medium Blue 8	Light Yellow 5	Medium Pink 2	Light Coral 3	Medium Blue 8	Light Blue 7

EMBROIDERY STITCH AND COLOR HEART 2

Inner edge		Outer edge								Inside square			
Border row stitch/color	Detail stitch/color	Rickrack and tatted lace/color			Border row stitch/color	Decorative stitch/color	Decorative stitch/color	Detail stitch/color		Border row stitch/color		Detail stitch/color	
Blanket stitch	3-wrap French knot stitch	3-wrap French knot stitch			Feather and chain stitch single	Lazy daisy stitch	Fly stitch	3-wrap French knot stitch		Cretan stitch		3-wrap French knot stitch	
Medium Green 10	Light Yellow 5	Medium Blue 8	Light Coral 3	Light Yellow 5	Light Green 10	Medium Pink 2	Light Blue 8	Medium Yellow 6		Light Pink 1	Medium Coral 4	Medium Blue 8	Light Blue 7

EMBROIDERY STITCH AND COLOR RICKRACK ROW

Rickrack/color		Decorative stitch/color	Detail stitch/color	Decorative stitch/color	Detail stitch/color	
Loop stitch leaves and stalk		Rosette	Single bead stitch	Lazy daisy stitch	3-wrap French knot stitch	
Medium Green 10	Light Green 9	Yellow Ombré 12	Medium Green 11	Light Blue 7	Medium Coral 4	Light Coral 3

Embroidered Trims

Trimmed seam embroidery is similar to straight-seam embroidery, with ribbon, lace, trim, or cords stitched over a seam or several seams. Ribbons or lengths of lace can be used to create a frame within a pieced design or to cover the raw edges of seams. I find these extra components helpful in hiding construction boo-boos that can occur in piecing (at least in my work). A whole section of lace, mesh, or netting can also be used to create an overall base design. The embroidery stitches are worked off of, or around, these components.

This project started with a Tentakulum silk hanky (an unraveled silk cocoon or silk roving),

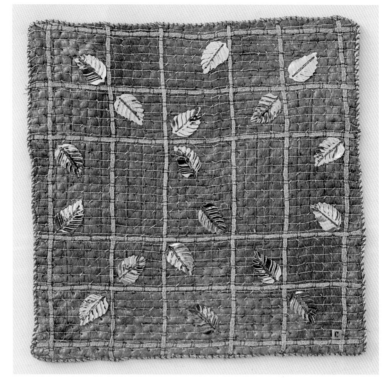

Enmeshed, 8″ × 8″

which was predyed in reds and greens. The silk square was first machine quilted in a Sulky metallic green thread. Vintage gold milliner's mesh was added as an additional color component and hand stitched to the silk base with green and red Kreinik metallic threads. Kreinik braid and cord was hand couched into sections and the outer edges of the uneven base. Sequins were stitched with a strand of DMC metallic floss. This piece was entirely embroidered with metallic threads.

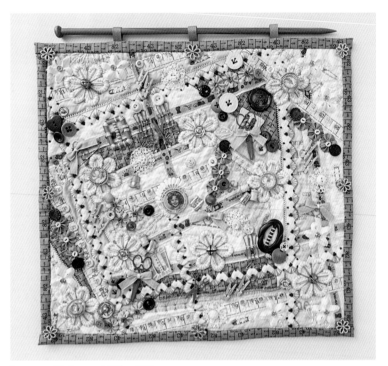

This monochromatic color palette combines a very subtle blend of cream, sand, tan, and brown. The fabrics are all scraps from other projects, with leftovers of ribbon, trims, and zippers for embellishments. I literally emptied the sewing box of snaps and hooks and eyes, combining these with charms and vintage buttons. The embroidery stitches were all worked in perle cotton.

Scraps and Leftovers, 14⅝″ × 15⅝″

This project started with a commercially embroidered piece of fabric that I used for the appliquéd teapot shape in the center. I found hand-dyed variegated perle cotton in the yellow, pink, and green colorway, which gave me the idea for the colors. I chose silk fabrics in those colors for the straight- and strip-pieced sections. I added trims to the seams and the edge of the appliqué shape, using yellow soutache, green leaf trim, and green satin ribbon. I added the cream lace and appliqués as an accent color. The embroidery was worked in light, medium, and dark tones of the three colors in perle cotton and cotton floss.

Chrysanthemum Tea, 14⅜″ × 14⅜″

Blue Lilies

FINISHED SIZE: 11¾″ × 11¾″

This slightly wonky strip-pieced base is made from silk and moiré fabrics with hand-dyed laces and strips. The strips of fabric were worked alternating between trimmed seam embroidery and straight-seam embroidery. The straight seams were minimally embroidered in order to highlight the trimmed sections and vignettes.

KEY ELEMENTS

Fabrics: raw silk, moiré, rayon lace and appliqués, cotton appliqué, silk satin ribbon, ¼" satin ribbon

Construction: trimmed and strip-pieced seams

Color discipline: Four Square (page 58)

Embroidery and embellishment materials: 4 mm silk embroidery ribbon; silk perle #8 and #12; rayon twisted thread #8; cotton floss; Chinese knotting cord; seed beads; acrylic flower bead; glass flower rondelles, flowers, leaves, and buttons

COLOR CODE

Fabric: Blue Silk 1, Teal Moiré 2, Green Moiré 3

Silk perle #8: Green 3a, Plum 4a

Twisted rayon thread: Teal 2b

2 strands of cotton floss: Blue 1c, Green 3c, Plum 4c

4 mm silk embroidery ribbon: Blue 1d, Teal 2d

Ribbon: Plum 4e

Cord: Teal 2f

Size 11 seed beads: Blue 1g, Teal 2g, Green 3g, Plum 4g

Glass buttons: Green 3h, Alexandrite 5h

Large beads: Purple 6i 12 mm flower, Green 3i 8 mm flower rondelle, Orchid 6i acrylic 16 mm flower and size 6 seed bead, Teal 2i 10 mm flower bead, Alexandrite 5i 14 mm leaf, Plum 4i tulip bead

TRIMMED SEAM EMBROIDERY STITCH AND COLOR DIAGRAM

Fabric	Border row stitch/color		Decorative stitch/color		Detail stitch/color	
Blue Silk 1 with Green Lace 3 and Teal 3 satin ribbon	Fly stitch side by side	Chain stitch	Stacked bead stitch		2-wrap French knot stitch	Single bead stitch
	Teal 2b	Green 3a	Orchid 6i	Green 3g	Green 3c	Plum 4g
Teal Moiré 1 with Blue Lace 1	Stacked bead stitch		Stacked bead stitch		Single bead stitch	
	Orchid 6i	Green 3g	Green 3i	Plum 4g	Alexandrite 5i	Green 3h
Green Moiré 2 with Plum Lace 4	Couched stitch		Couched stitch		Stitched buttons	
	Blue 1d	Green 3c	Teal 2f	Green 3c	Green 3h, Alexandrite 5h	

STRAIGHT SEAM EMBROIDERY STITCH AND COLOR DIAGRAM

Fabric	Border row stitch/color	Decorative stitch	Detail stitch
Blue Silk 1	Blanket stitch	Fly stitch	Single bead stitch
	Teal 2b	Green 3c	Plum 4g
Teal Moiré 2	Cretan stitch	Lazy daisy stitch	Single bead stitch
	Green 3a	Plum 4c	Blue 1g
Green Moiré 3	Looped feather stitch	Fly stitch	Single bead stitch
	Plum 4a	Blue 1c	Teal 2g

VIGNETTE EMBROIDERY STITCH AND COLOR DIAGRAM

Large component	Decorative stitch		Lazy daisy stitch	3-wrap French knot stitch	Detail stitches				
	Couched stitch				Stacked bead stitch			Single bead stitch	
Rosette	Teal 2f	Green 3c	Teal 2d	Blue 1d	Plum 4i/ Blue 1g	Purple 6i/ Green 3g	Green 3i/ Blue 1g	Teal 2i	Alexandrite 5i
Plum Ribbon 4e									

Shadow Embroidery

Shadow embroidery follows a shape, such as a button, piece of lace, or a design in the fabric. The design is worked in a continuous row around the shape, using one stitch or several stitches. The embroidery rows grow in size, expanding upon the original design. A single design or shape can be stitched, or several designs can be stitched; these stitches can be left as separate components, or they can eventually be con-

Spring Butterflies, 3¼" × 6¾"

nected. This type of embroidery can be worked in a continuous border row stitch such as the blanket, chain, or feather stitch. Decorative and detail stitches such as the shell, lazy daisy, and French knot stitches can be worked between corners or other shapes to fill out the design.

The base of the fabric was strip pieced in two colors of silk fabric. Strips of vintage lace were stitched down the seams and in the center of the back section to create a design element. Vintage butterfly appliqués were stitched to the center flap and the inside front flap. The embroidery stitches were worked off of the butterfly shapes and the lace edges in four colors of Wildflowers variegated threads. A vintage glass button was used for the closure.

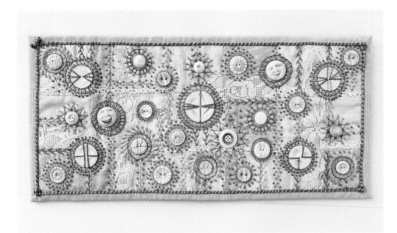

Bouncing Button Balloons, 7⅝" × 16¼"

Scraps of silk and bengaline fabrics ranging from dusty sand to a golden yellow were randomly strip pieced with vintage lace trim to add another design element. The embroidery stitches are focused around the vintage celluloid and fabric buttons that were stitched at key points throughout the base. Three subtle colorways of Wildflowers threads and size 11 seed beads were used for the embroidery stitches.

Sand Pebbles, 8" × 8½"

This piece started with a beautiful vintage lace appliqué that was given to me by a friend. I found a sand-colored cotton fabric for the background and a piece of Hanah silk ribbon from my collection that gave me the cream, brown, and deep brown colors of a striped shell. I found three colors of Wildflowers threads that picked up these colors, also introducing a light pink-and-gray tone. Vintage blown-glass beads, silver jewelry findings, and seed beads embellish the piece.

Mystic Twilight

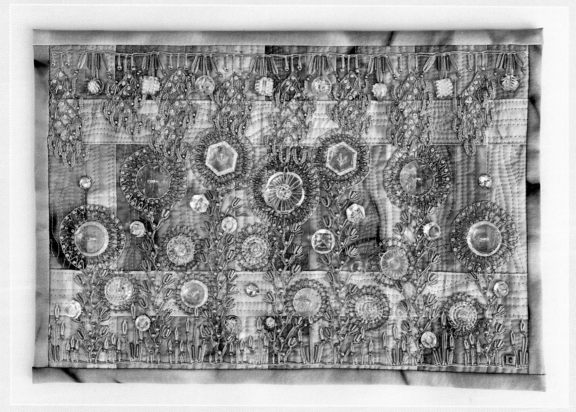

FINISHED SIZE: 9″ × 13¼″

I chose the pattern and colors of the strip-pieced batik background to simulate a worn wooden fence. I machine quilted each strip with a wood grain pattern. I chose large clear glass buttons in a variety of sizes for the flower centers. The outline of the large- and medium-sized buttons were shadowed with thread and bead embroidery; the border row stitches that represent grass and vines were worked in perle cotton and then shadowed with the same stitch in cotton floss.

KEY ELEMENTS

Fabrics: cotton batiks

Construction: strip pieced, machine quilted with Sulky metallic thread

Color discipline: Piggyback Jack (page 70)

Embroidery and embellishment materials: Finca perle cotton #8, Anchor perle cotton #12, Finca and DMC cotton floss, Finca metallic floss, glass seed and bugle beads, vintage buttons

COLOR CODE

Perle cotton #8: Variegated 1a, Sage 2a, Blue 3a, Beige 4a, Rose 5a

Perle cotton #12: Plum 6a

Cotton floss and metallic floss: Sage 2b, Blue 3b, Beige 4b, Plum 6b, Silver 7b

Size 11 seed beads: Sage 2c, Blue 3c, Plum 6c

Additional beads: Sage 2d bugle bead, Rose 5d size 8 seed bead, Plum 6d bugle bead

Buttons: clear

EMBROIDERY STITCH AND COLOR DIAGRAM

Rows	Border row stitch		Decorative stitch		Detail stitch			
Border grass (bottom edge)	Blanket stitch short-long-short	Shadowed blanket stitch short-long-short	Lazy daisy stitch	Shadowed lazy daisy stitch	Single bead stitch			
	Blue 3a	Sage 2b	Beige 4a	Plum 6a	Blue 3c		Sage 2d	
Flower stalk	Feather stitch	Shadowed feather stitch	Fly stitch	Lazy daisy stitch	3-wrap French knot stitch		Single bead stitch	
	Sage 2a	Blue 3b	Rose 5a	Variegated 1a	Plum 6b		Rose 5d	Plum 6d
Large button flowers	Lazy daisy stitch row	Chain stitch	Blanket stitch	Fly stitch row	3-wrap French knot stitch	2-wrap French knot stitch		Single bead stitch
	Rose 5a		Plum 6a	Variegated 1a	Variegated 1a	Beige 4b		Plum 6c
Medium button flowers	Lazy daisy stitch row	Chain stitch	Blanket stitch		3-wrap French knot stitch			
	Rose 5a		Plum 6a		Variegated 1a			
Small button flowers	Continuous bead stitch row							
	Blue 3c							
Border vine (top edge)	Blanket stitch short-long-short	Shadowed blanket stitch short-long-short	Stitched buttons		Single bead stitch		Grouped bead stitch	
	Blue 3a	Sage 2b	Silver 7b		Sage 2d	Rose 5d	Blue 3c	
Hanging vine	Feather stitch random	Shadowed feather stitch random	Frilled petal stitch	Lazy daisy stitch	3-wrap French knot stitch		Single bead stitch	
	Sage 2a	Blue 3b	Rose 5a	Plum 6a / Variegated 1a	Beige 4a	Sage 2c		Plum 6c

Bordered Designs

Bordered designs can follow an imaginary line on a solid background or a seam on a pieced project. A pieced project can have some strips entirely filled in with embroidery and other strips with only minimal embroidery. You can work the border row first, filling in with decorative and detail stitches, or work the large components first, followed by the medium components, the small components, and then any detail stitches.

The spiral border was machine stitched in a free-form pattern with a variegated cotton sewing thread. The design started in the center with five flower designs, each with a stalk and leaf worked

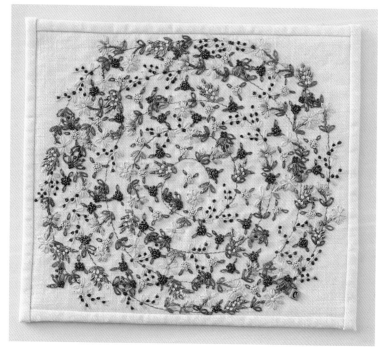

Merrily We Go Around, 6¾″ × 7¾″

along the row. After this group, one of two vine designs was stitched in. The pattern then repeats itself. Small flowers were interspersed here and there to fill in the background.

Sweet Roses and Posies, 8¼″ × 8¼″

This project features strip-pieced cotton batik fabric with the embroidery stitches worked into individual vignettes following the outer and inner edges of the seams. The color theory application is Follow the Leader (page 74), with the base row stitches embroidered in one color of Wildflowers thread and the decorative and detail stitches worked in six colors of silk embroidery ribbon and silk floss.

Fields of Gold, 8½″ round

I pieced yellow and black silk triangles into a square with a center and outer circle of black lace that provided the border for the embroidered designs. The antique porcelain button in the center was the inspiration for the yellow and black color choices; the hint of green provided an accent color. The project is embellished with vintage and newer glass, plastic, and celluloid buttons; ribbonwork flowers made from ¼″ picot-edged ombré ribbon; vintage and new ⅜″ grosgrain ribbon; and glass beads. It was embroidered with 4 mm and 7 mm silk embroidery ribbon, perle cotton #8 and #12, variegated rayon twisted thread, and cotton floss. Silk rouleau cord was hand stitched to the outer edge.

California Dreamin'

FINISHED SIZE: 11¼″ × 11¼″

This project started with a simple strip-pieced design using two marbled fabrics and bleached muslin. The center and third row were cut from bleached muslin and were then entirely embroidered with decorative and detail stitches. The second and fourth rows were cut from the two marbled fabrics, with each strip bordered with chain and French knot stitches. Vintage glass beads provide an accent.

KEY ELEMENTS

Fabrics: cotton muslin and marbled cotton

Construction: strip pieced

Color discipline: Colors and More Colors (page 66)

Embroidery and embellishment materials: perle cotton #5, cotton floss, vintage glass beads

COLOR CODE

Perle cotton #5: Light Purple 2a, Turquoise 3a, Ombré Green 4a, Pink 5a

Cotton floss: Variegated 1b (pink, orange, yellow, blue, green), Dark Purple 2b, Ombré Turquoise 3b, Ombré Green 4b, Ombré Pink 5b, Ombré Coral 6b, Yellow 7b, Lime Green 8b, Variegated 9b (turquoise, pink, green)

EMBROIDERY STITCH AND COLOR DIAGRAM

Row	Large component		Medium component				Small component				
Muslin square and Row 3	Gwen's rose stitch		Jill's flower stitch	3-wrap French knot stitch	Lazy daisy stitch flower	3-wrap French knot stitch	Lazy daisy stitch	French knot flower stitch		Fly stitch side by side	
	Turquoise 3a	Variegated 9b	Ombré Coral 6b	Ombré Pink 5b	Ombré Pink 5b	Dark Purple 2b	Ombré Green 4b	Pink 5a		Ombré Coral 6b	
	Buttonhole circle stitch	5-wrap French knot stitch	Barnacle stitch	2-wrap French knot stitch	Whipstitch star	Lazy daisy stitch	3-wrap French knot stitch				
	Light Purple 2a	Pink 5a	Lime Green 8b	Ombré Turquoise 3b	Ombré Turquoise 3b	Ombré Green 4a	Dark Purple 2b	Ombré Pink 5b	Ombré Green 4b	Yellow 7b	Lime Green 8b
Row 2 and 4	Chain stitch		3-wrap French knot stitch								
	Lime Green 8b		Variegated 1b								

Vignette Designs

Vignette embroidery is worked in small sections with large, medium, and small components and detail stitches. You can work vignettes in sections on a solid background of a fabric base or in sections of a pieced base. The colors of vignettes should complement all of the fabrics. If you are using more than one vignette, repeat the design in a balanced fashion so that the colors flow.

silk embroidery ribbon and cotton floss. Vintage mother-of-pearl buttons and glass beads were used as embellishments. Further embellishments include vintage embroidered and lace appliqués, and ribbon-work flowers made from vintage and new ombré, velvet, and taffeta ribbons.

For Elizabeth, 7¼" round

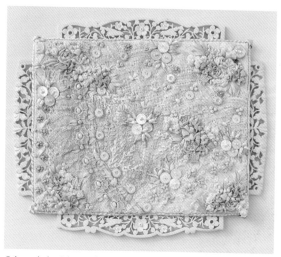

Crème de la Crème, 9" × 10¾"

This project started with a vintage batiste handkerchief and two colors of moiré fabric. Hand-dyed vintage lace was stitched to create a border for the vignettes and embroidery stitches. The embroidery stitches were worked in 2 mm, 4 mm, and 7 mm

The background fabric is a doupioni silk, with lace fabrics, collars, and trims appliquéd in a crazy-pieced pattern. The lace was hand stitched in place first. Then the ribbon trim was stitched down and used to cover any raw edges and to create a design detail. The embroidered vignettes include ribbonwork flowers and flowers stitched in three sizes of silk embroidery ribbon. Beads and buttons were added to the vignettes and sprinkled throughout the overall design.

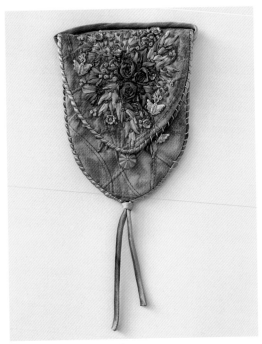

Dried Roses Purse, 4¾″ × 4″

Detail of purse front flap

Detail of purse back

Detail of purse front under flap

The cotton batik fabric for the base of the purse was randomly machine quilted using a double needle and metallic thread. The vignette embroidery stitches were worked in solid and hand-dyed 4 mm silk embroidery ribbon. Glass beads and metal charms embellish the purse.

Charlotte's Webs

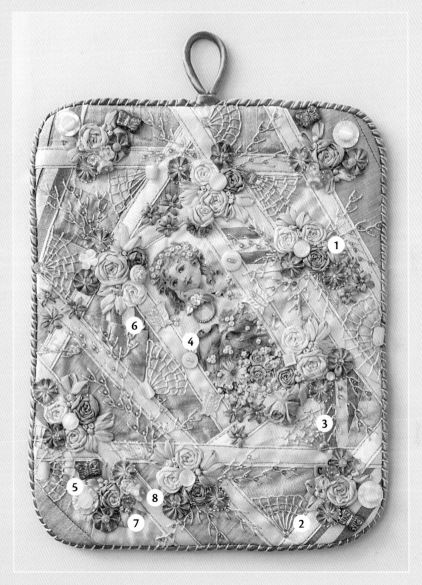

FINISHED SIZE: 8½″ × 7″

This project started with the little girl in the center of the piece, whom I named Charlotte. The center section was crazy pieced with tiny and tinier pieces of leftover silk scraps. Satin ribbon was machine stitched randomly to create sections for the vignette embroidery, which was worked in silk embroidery ribbon and perle cotton. Vintage glass and mother-of-pearl buttons were added here and there with glass beads and charms.

KEY ELEMENTS

Fabrics: silk fabric scraps, printed cigar silk

Construction: crazy pieced with satin ribbon sections

Color discipline: Colors and More Colors (page 66)

Embroidery and embellishment materials: 2 mm, 4 mm, and 7 mm silk embroidery ribbon; ¼" ombré ribbon; Finca perle cotton #8; size 6 and 11 seed beads; vintage mother-of-pearl and glass buttons; 3 mm Czech bead; glass flower and butterfly beads; glass flower buttons; 6 mm rondelle; vintage mother-of-pearl butterfly charm

COLOR CODE

7 mm silk embroidery ribbon: Yellow 1a, Purple 2a, Peach 3a

4 mm silk embroidery ribbon: Lavender 4b, Sea Green 5b, Chamois 6b

¼" ombré ribbon: Orchid 7c, Periwinkle/Pink 9c

Finca perle cotton #8: Sea Green 5d, Chamois 6d, Light Purple 8d

Size 11 seed beads: Peach 3e, Sea Green 5e, Light Purple 8e

Larger beads: Yellow 1f size 6 seed bead, Chamois 6f 6 mm rondelle, Peach 3f 3 mm Czech bead

Size 15 seed bead: Sea Green 5g

Buttons and beads: Yellow 1g flower button, Peach 3g flower bead, Mother-of-Pearl 10g button, Pink 11g button, Butterscotch 12g button, Green AB 13g butterfly bead

Charms: Mother-of-Pearl 10h butterfly charm

EMBROIDERY STITCH AND COLOR DIAGRAM VIGNETTE 1

Large components			Detail stitch
Woven rose stitch	Woven rose stitch	Woven rose stitch	Stitched button
Yellow 1a	Purple 2a	Peach 3a	Mother-of-Pearl 10g
Ribbonwork flowers			
Rosette	Stacked bead stitch	Rosette	Stacked bead stitch
Orchid 7c	Peach 3f / Sea Green 5g	Periwinkle/Pink 9c	Yellow 1f / Peach 3e
Medium component	Small component	Medium component	Small component
Lazy daisy stitch	3-wrap French knot stitch	Straight stitch flower	Single bead stitch
Sea Green 5b	Chamois 6b	Lavender 4b	Peach 3e
Medium component	Small components		
Vine: feather stitch	Single bead stitch		
Sea Green 5d	Peach 3e	Sea Green 5e	Light Purple 8e

EMBROIDERY STITCH AND COLOR DIAGRAM VIGNETTE 2

Large component			Small component
Blanket stitch cobweb			Single bead stitch
Sea Green 5d	Chamois 6d	Light Purple 8d	Yellow 1f

EMBROIDERY STITCH AND COLOR DIAGRAM VIGNETTE 3

Large component		Small component
Frilly spider web		Stitched button
Sea Green 5d	Light Purple 8d	Butterscotch 12g

EMBROIDERY STITCH AND COLOR DIAGRAM ADDITIONAL DETAILS

Detail stitches			
4. 3-wrap French knot stitch	5. Single bead stitch	6. Bead cascade stitch	
Chamois 6d	Green AB 13g	Mother-of-Pearl 10h	Sea Green 5g
7. Stitched button		8. Stacked bead stitch	
Yellow 1g	Pink 11g	Peach 3g	Sea Green 5g

Overall Design

An overall design covers an entire area, such as a wholecloth base or sections of a strip-pieced base. The embroidery design can start with an appliqué base of bits of lace to create a basket for a floral arrangement. The embroidery design can also be worked in a random-appearing design to fill in a solid piece or section of fabric.

This little square was sectioned into a grid pattern to create small, evenly spaced vignettes. I couched silk embroidery ribbon and chain stitches to create the grid. The vignettes were stitched with decorative and detail stitches.

Flower Child, 5¾" × 6½"

Two batik fabrics were strip pieced together with a V-shaped section ending at the tip of the heart-shaped base. The embroidered flowers and leaves were worked in silk embroidery ribbon, silk floss, and buttonhole twist. Sequins, glass beads, buttons, and flower-shaped rondelles were added for details. Rayon cord was couched to the outer edge.

Serendipity, 6¼" × 6⅝"

This piece started with two small sections of hand-dyed silk fabrics—one solid and one variegated in color—that I strip pieced into a square. I combined the fabric with silk embroidery ribbons and threads left over from various other projects. The background fabric is in medium tones and the silk embroidery ribbons in light, medium, and dark tones. Glass beads glisten here and there.

Cancun Dreams, 9" × 7¾"

Tatiana's Garden

FINISHED SIZE: 10˝ × 8¼˝

This project started with a solid piece of tone-on-tone woven cotton print fabric with a floral pattern. I randomly machine stitched the fabric with an ombré green cotton thread. Two vintage lace cuffs, lace yardage, and appliqués were hand stitched to create a basket with a handle. Silk embroidery ribbon was stitched in yellow, purple, fuchsia, and shades of green. I added vintage glass buttons, glass charms, and seed beads to accent the embroidery.

KEY ELEMENTS

Fabrics: jacquard cotton upholstery fabric; vintage lace cuff, partial collar, and lace trim

Construction: appliqué, whole cloth with machine-quilted lines

Color discipline: Five and Dime (page 62)

Embroidery and embellishment materials: 4 mm and 7 mm silk embroidery ribbon, ¼" ombré ribbon, buttonhole twist, twisted rayon #8, perle cotton #12, cotton floss, size 6 and 11 seed beads, vintage glass buttons, glass butterfly

COLOR CODE

7 mm silk embroidery ribbon: Yellow 1a, Purple 2a, Fuchsia 3a, Lime Green 4, Apple Green 5

4 mm silk embroidery ribbon: Purple 2b, Fuchsia 3b, Ombré Green 6b

Threads: Yellow 1c buttonhole twist, Purple 2c buttonhole twist, Fuchsia 3c rayon twist, Ombré Green 6c perle cotton #12

Size 11 seed beads: Yellow 1d, Purple 2d, Fuchsia 3d, Lime Green 4d, Apple Green 5d

Size 6 seed bead: Yellow 1e

Button: Apple Green 5f

EMBROIDERY STITCH AND COLOR DIAGRAM CENTER VIGNETTE 1

Large component			Medium component	Small component	Detail stitch	
Mum stitch			Lazy daisy stitch	Accordion rose stitch	Stacked bead stitch	
Fuchsia 3a	Fuchsia 3b	Fuchsia 3c	Apple Green 5a	Yellow 1a	Yellow 1e	Lime Green 4d
Hyacinth: 5-wrap, 4-wrap, and 3-wrap French knot stitch			Lazy daisy stitch		Single bead stitch	
Purple 2a			Ombré Green 6b		Yellow 1d	

EMBROIDERY STITCH AND COLOR DIAGRAM CENTER VIGNETTE 2

Large component		Medium component		Detail stitch	
Vine: ribbon stitch		Lazy daisy knot tip stitch	Lazy daisy stitch	3-wrap French knot stitch	Single bead stitch
Lime Green 4a	Ombré Green 6b	Purple 2b	Yellow 1c	Fuchsia 3a	Lime Green 4d

EMBROIDERY STITCH AND COLOR DIAGRAM CENTER VIGNETTE 3

Medium component	Small component	Decorative stitch	Detail stitch	
Lazy daisy stitch	Accordion rose stitch	Grouped bead stitch	Stacked bead stitch	
Apple Green 5a	Yellow 1a	Lime Green 4d	Yellow 1e	Lime Green 4d

EMBROIDERY STITCH AND COLOR DIAGRAM FERNS, VINES, AND BUTTONS

4. Fern			5. Fern		
Chain stitch	Straight stitch	Single bead stitch	Chain stitch	Lazy daisy bullion tip stitch	3-wrap French knot stitch
Ombré Green 6c	Lime Green 4a	Fuchsia 3d	Ombré Green 6c	Fuchsia 3b	Purple 2c
6. Fern			**7. Fern**		
Chain stitch	Ribbon stitch	Single bead stitch	Chain stitch	Lazy daisy bullion tip stitch	Ribbon stitch	3-wrap French knot stitch
Ombré Green 6c	Ombré Green 6b	Purple 2d	Ombré Green 6c	Fuchsia 3b	Ombré Green 6b	Fuchsia 3c
8. Vine		**9. Vine**		**10. Beaded button**	
Chain stitch	Grouped bead stitch	Chain stitch	Grouped bead stitch	Picot tip stitch	
Ombré Green 6c	Purple 2d	Ombré Green 6c	Fuchsia 3d	Apple Green 5f	Yellow 1d

EMBROIDERY AND EMBELLISHMENT
STITCH REFERENCE GUIDE

Victoriana, side 2, 9¼″ × 9¼″

The following directions will list the suggested threads, silk embroidery ribbons, woven ribbons, beads, or other embellishments that are best suited for each technique. See All the Right Stuff (page 13) for suggestions on which materials would be appropriate for your project. For suggested needles and other tips, see Embroidery Basics (page 154). For ideas on how to use the stitches in a design, refer to Embroider, Embellish, and Explore (page 78).

Blanket and Buttonhole Stitches

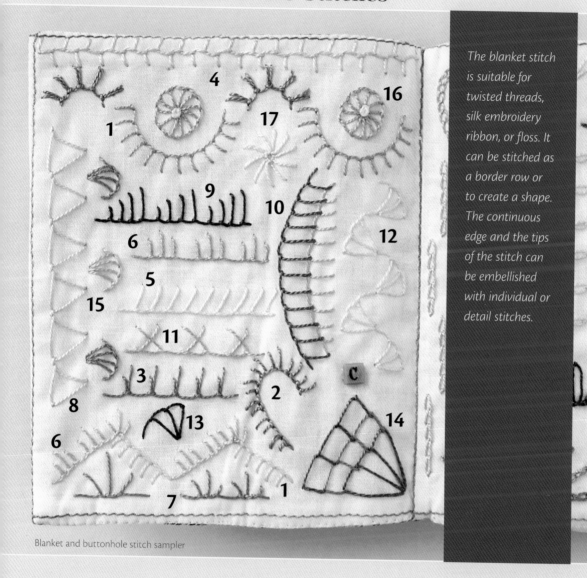

The blanket stitch is suitable for twisted threads, silk embroidery ribbon, or floss. It can be stitched as a border row or to create a shape. The continuous edge and the tips of the stitch can be embellished with individual or detail stitches.

Blanket and buttonhole stitch sampler

Border Row Stitches

1. Blanket Stitch (page 116)

2. Blanket Stitch Grouped Even (page 116)

3. Blanket Stitch Up and Down (page 116)

4. Blanket Stitch Zipper Row (page 116)

5. Blanket Stitch Angled (page 116)

6. Blanket Stitch Short-Long-Short (page 116)

7. Blanket Stitch Stalk (page 117)

8. Blanket Stitch Closed (page 117)

9. Musical Notes Stitch (page 117)

10. Blanket Stitch Dipped (page 117)

11. Blanket Stitch Crossed (page 117)

12. Shell Stitch Row (page 117)

Decorative Stitches

13. Shell Stitch (page 118)

14. Blanket Stitch Cobweb (page 118)

15. Bell Flower Stitch (page 118)

16. Buttonhole Circle Stitch (page 118)

17. Blanket Stitch Flower (page 118)

Blanket Stitch

1. Come up at **A**. *In one motion, go down at **B** and up at **C**. Loop the working thread under the tip of the needle. Pull the needle through the fabric.

2. To finish the row, repeat from *. To end the stitch, go down at **D**.

Blanket Stitch Grouped Even

Follow the steps of the blanket stitch (at left). Work a group of 2 stitches, leaving a space between groups.

Blanket Stitch Up and Down

1. *Follow Step 1 of the blanket stitch (at left).

2. In one motion, go down at **D** and up at **E**. Loop the working thread over the tip of the needle.

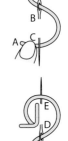

3. Pull the needle through the fabric. Thread the needle under the loop and gently pull the thread to tighten. To finish the row, repeat from *, leaving a space between groups. To end the stitch, go down at **F**.

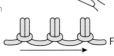

Blanket Stitch Zipper Row

1. Work the tips of this stitch along 2 imaginary parallel lines. Follow Step 1 of the blanket stitch (above).

2. Go down at **D** and up at **E**, looping the working thread under the tip of the needle. Pull the needle through the fabric.

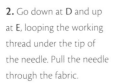

3. To finish the row, repeat Steps 1 and 2, alternating the direction of the stitches. To end the stitch, go down at **F**.

Blanket Stitch Angled

1. Follow Step 1 of the blanket stitch (above left), *with the stitch angled right to left.

2. To finish the row, repeat from *. To end the stitch, go down at **D**.

Blanket Stitch Short-Long-Short

Follow the steps of the blanket stitch (above left). Work a group of stitches with their tips altered from short to long to short. Leave a space between groups.

Blanket Stitch Stalk

1. Follow Step 1 of the blanket stitch (previous page), with the stitch angled left to right.

2. Work a second stitch straight. Work a third stitch angled right to left. To end the stitch, go down at **D** a short distance away.

Blanket Stitch Closed

1. Follow Step 1 of the blanket stitch (previous page), *with the stitch angled right to left.

2. Work a second stitch, going down at **B** and up at **D**, with the stitch angled left to right.

3. To finish the row, repeat from *. To end the stitch, go down at **E** a short distance from **D**.

Musical Notes Stitch

Follow the steps of the blanket stitch (previous page). Work a group of 4–5 stitches, starting with the first tip short and then gradually increasing the size.

Blanket Stitch Dipped

Draw a curved line to follow. Follow the steps of the blanket stitch (previous page), with **A** and **C** worked on the line.

Blanket Stitch Crossed

1. Follow Step 1 of the blanket stitch (previous page), *with the stitch angled right to left.

2. Work a second stitch, going down at **D** and up at **E**, with the stitch angled left to right and crossed over the previous stitch.

3. To finish the row, repeat from *. To end the stitch, go down at **F**.

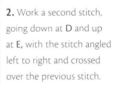

Shell Stitch Row

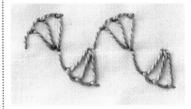

Follow the steps of the shell stitch (page 118). Work the stitches on either side of a seam or line.

Shell Stitch

1. Draw or follow a quarter-circle. Follow Step 1 of the blanket stitch (page 116), with **A** and **C** on the line.

2. Work a second stitch and a third stitch along the curved line. To end the stitch, go down at **D**.

Blanket Stitch Cobweb

1. Follow the steps for the shell stitch (at left); work a complete stitch.

2. Draw or follow a line slightly above the curve of the previous row. Follow Step 1 of the blanket stitch (page 116), with **A** and **C** on the line and **B** inside the first stitch of the previous row.

3. Work a second and third stitch. To end the stitch, go down at **D**.

Straight stitch

4. Follow Steps 2 and 3 above to work a third row of stitches into the second row of stitches. Work a straight stitch at the beginning of each row of stitches.

Bell Flower Stitch

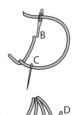

1. Draw or follow a half-circle and mark a center point. Follow Step 1 of the blanket stitch (page 116), *with **B** as the center point and **A** and **C** on the curved line.

2. Repeat from *, working the stitches around the curve.

3. To end the stitch, go down at **D** a slight distance from **C**.

Buttonhole Circle Stitch

1. Draw or follow a circle and mark the center point. Follow Step 1 of the blanket stitch (page 116), *with **B** as the center point and **A** and **C** on the curved line.

2. Repeat from *, working around the circle.

3. To end the stitch, go down next to the first stitch.

Blanket Stitch Flower

1. Draw a small circle. Follow Step 1 of the blanket stitch (page 116), *with **A** and **C** on the curved line.

2. Repeat from *, working around the circle.

3. To end the stitch, go down at **D** next to **A**.

First stitch

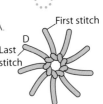

Last stitch

Chain and Looped Stitches

The chain stitch is suitable for twisted threads, floss, or silk embroidery ribbon. It can be stitched as a border row or to create a shape.

Chain and looped stitch sampler

Border Row Stitches

1. Chain Stitch (page 120)

2. Chain Stitch Zigzag (page 120)

3. Chain Stitch Double (page 120)

4. Chain Stitch Open (page 120)

5. Chain Stitch Cable (page 120)

6. Chain Stitch Feathered (page 120)

7. Looped Blanket Stitch (page 121)

8. Looped Feather Stitch (page 121)

9. Loop Stitch Petal Row (page 121)

10. Loop Stitch Leaves and Stalk (page 121)

11. Looped Cretan Stitch (page 121)

12. Chain Stitch Loop (page 121)

Chain Stitch

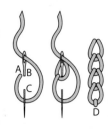

1. Come up through the fabric at **A**. *In one motion, go down at **B** and up at **C**. Loop the working thread under the tip of the needle. Pull the needle through the fabric.

2. To finish the row, repeat from *, starting inside the previous loop. To end the stitch, go down at **D**.

Chain Stitch Zigzag

Follow the directions for the chain stitch (at left); angle the first stitch away from the seam, and angle the next stitch toward the seam. Repeat angling the stitches from side to side.

Chain Stitch Double

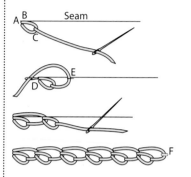

1. *Follow Step 1 of the chain stitch (at left), working the stitch slightly angled and next to the seam.

2. In one motion, go down at **D** next to **B** and up at **E** on the seam.

3. To finish the row, repeat from *, beginning inside the loop of the stitch in Step 2. To end the stitch, go down at **F**.

Chain Stitch Open

1. Work a chain stitch (above), with points **A** and **B** slightly apart.

2. In one motion, go down at **B** (outside the previous loop) and up at **C**. Repeat this step to finish the row. To end the stitch, go down at **D**.

Chain Stitch Cable

1. Come up through the fabric at **A**. *Wrap the thread over the needle once; this creates a 1-wrap French knot (page 133).

2. In one motion, go down at **B** and up at **C**. Loop the working thread under the tip of the needle; pull the knot close to the fabric. Pull the needle through the fabric.

3. To finish the row, repeat from *. To end the stitch, go down at **D**.

Chain Stitch Feathered

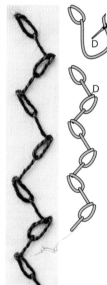

1. Follow Step 1 of the chain stitch (above left), angling the stitch away from the seam or line. Go down at **D** a short distance away.

2. Stitch the next stitch beginning at **D** of the previous stitch. Repeat, angling the stitches from side to side.

Looped Blanket Stitch

1. Come up at A. *In one motion, go down at B and up at C. Loop the working thread under the tip of the needle to the base of the stitch. Pull the thread through the fabric.

2. Go down at D to catch the loop. Come up at E.

3. To finish the row, repeat from * a short distance away. To end the stitch, go down at F.

Looped Feather Stitch

1. Come up at A. *Follow Step 1 and 2 of the looped blanket stitch (at left), working to the right.

2. Work the next stitch to the left. To finish the row, repeat from *, alternating the stitches from right to left. To end the stitch, go down at F.

Loop Stitch Petal Row

1. *Follow Steps 1 and 2 for the looped blanket stitch (at left), with the first stitch angled slightly to the left.

2. Work a second stitch straight up and a third stitch angled to the right.

3. To finish the row, repeat from * a short distance away. To end the stitch, go down at F.

Loop Stitch Leaves and Stalk

1. Follow Steps 1 and 2 for the looped blanket stitch (above), with the stitch angled slightly to the left.

2. In one motion, go down at F and up at G to stitch a straight blanket stitch.

3. Follow Step 1 above, with the stitch angled slightly to the right. To end the stitch, go down at H a short distance away.

Looped Cretan Stitch

1. Work this stitch along 2 imaginary parallel lines. *Follow Steps 1 and 2 of the looped blanket stitch (above left).

2. Work the next stitch below and to the right of the first.

3. To finish the row, repeat from *, alternating the direction of the stitches. To end the stitch, go down at F.

Chain Stitch Loop

Follow the directions for the chain stitch (previous page), working the stitch in a curved loop.

Chevron, Cretan, Cross, and Herringbone Stitches

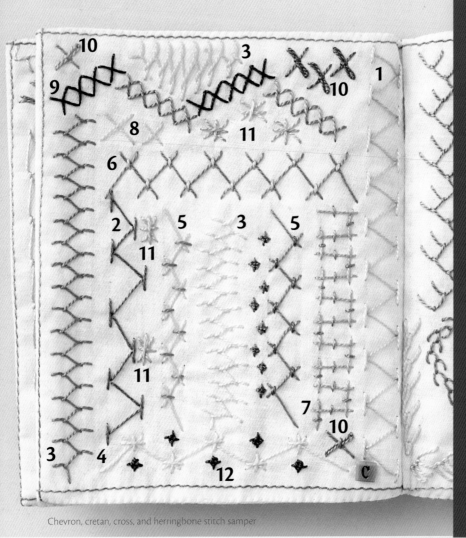

The chevron, cretan, and herringbone stitches can be stitched as a border row; the cross stitch can be stitched as a single unit or as a border row. The tips of the stitch can be embellished with individual or detail stitches. These stitches are suitable for twisted threads, silk embroidery ribbon, or floss.

Chevron, cretan, cross, and herringbone stitch samper

Border Row Stitches

1. Chevron Stitch (page 123)

2. Chevron Stitch Short-Long (page 123)

3. Cretan Stitch (page 123)

4. Herringbone Stitch (page 123)

5. Herringbone Stitch Elongated or Widened (page 123)

6. Herringbone Stitch Detailed (page 123)

7. Herringbone Stitch Boxed (page 124)

9. Cross Stitch Row (page 124)

Decorative Stitches

8. Cross Stitch (page 124)

10. Crossed Loop Stitch (page 124)

11. Star Stitch (page 124)

12. Celtic Knot Stitch (page 124)

Chevron Stitch

1. Work this stitch along 2 imaginary parallel lines. Come up at **A**. In one motion, go down at **B** and up at **C**. Pull the needle through the fabric.

2. *In one motion, go down at **D** and up at **E**. Pull the needle through the fabric.

3. In one motion, go down at **F** and up at **D**.

4. To finish the row, repeat from *, alternating the stitches from row to row. To end the stitch, go down at **F**.

Chevron Stitch Short-Long

Follow the directions for the chevron stitch (at left), working the bottom row along one line and the top row along two different lines.

Cretan Stitch

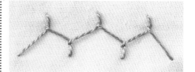

1. Work the tips of this stitch along 2 imaginary parallel lines. Come up at **A**. *In one motion, go down at **B** and up at **C**, looping the working thread under the tip of the needle. Pull the needle through the fabric.

2. In one motion, go down at **D** and up at **E**, looping the working thread under the tip of the needle. Pull the needle through the fabric.

3. To finish the row, repeat from *. To end the stitch, go down at **F**.

Herringbone Stitch

1. Work this stitch along 2 imaginary parallel lines. Come up at **A**. *In one motion, go down at **B** and up at **C**. Pull the needle through the fabric.

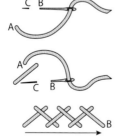

2. To finish the row, repeat from *, stitching on alternate lines. To end the stitch, go down at **B**.

Herringbone Stitch Elongated or Widened

Elongated: work a row of herringbone stitches (at left) that are longer and closer together. Widened: work a row of herringbone stitches that are shorter and wider apart.

Herringbone Stitch Detailed

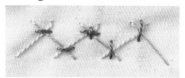

Work a row of herringbone stitches (at left). Come back with the same thread or a different color and add straight stitch (page 132) details as shown.

Herringbone Stitch Boxed

1. *Come up at A. In one motion, go down at B and up at C. Pull the needle through the fabric and go down at D.

2. Come up at E. In one motion, go down at F and up at G. Pull the needle through the fabric and go down at H.

3. To finish the row, repeat from *. To end the stitch, go down at D or H.

Cross Stitch

1. Come up at A and go down at B.

2. Come up at C and go down at D.

Cross Stitch Row

1. Come up at A. *In one motion, go down at B and up at C. Pull the needle through the fabric. To finish the row, repeat from *.

2. **In one motion, go down at D and up at E. Pull the needle through the fabric.

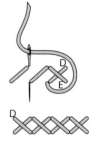

3. Repeat from **, working to the beginning of the row. To end the stitch, go down at D.

Crossed Loop Stitch

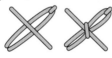

1. Work a lazy daisy stitch (page 135).

2. Work a straight stitch (page 132) the same length and width over the lazy daisy.

3. Work a short straight stitch across the middle of the crossed section.

Star Stitch

1. Work a cross stitch (above).

2. Work a second cross stitch in the same color or a different color.

Celtic Knot Stitch

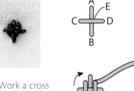

1. Work a cross stitch (above center). Come up at E.

2. Working counterclockwise, cross the thread over the length at D, under the length at B, over the length at C, and under the length at A.

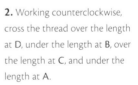

3. To end the stitch, go down at E.

Feather Stitches

The feather stitch is suitable for twisted threads, silk embroidery ribbon, or floss. It can be stitched as a border row or to create a shape. The tips of the stitch can be embellished with individual or detail stitches.

Feather stitch sampler

Border Row Stitches

1. Feather Stitch (page 126)

2. Feather Stitch Double (page 126)

3. Feather Stitch Random (page 126)

4. Feather Stitch Straight Center (page 126)

5. Feather Stitch Single (page 126)

6. Feather Stitch Piggyback (page 126)

7. Feather Stitch Closed (page 126)

8. Maidenhair Fern Stitch (page 127)

9. Maidenhair Fern Stitch Single (page 127)

10. Feather and Chain Stitch (page 127)

11. Feather and Chain Stitch Variation (page 127)

12. Feather and Chain Stitch Single (page 127)

Feather Stitch

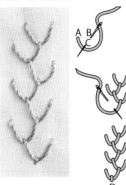

1. Come up at **A**. *In one motion, go down at **B** and up at **C**. Loop the working thread under the tip of the needle. Pull the needle through the fabric.

2. Repeat from *, working the next stitch below and to the left.

3. Repeat Steps 1 and 2 to finish the row. To end the stitch, go down at **D**.

Feather Stitch Double

1. Follow Step 1 of the feather stitch (at left). Work a second stitch below and to the right.

2. Follow Step 2 of the feather stitch. Work a second stitch below and to the left.

3. Repeat Steps 1 and 2, alternating 2 stitches to the right and to the left. To end the stitch, go down at **D**.

Feather Stitch Random

Follow the directions for the feather stitch (at left), working stitches to the right and to the left in random amounts.

Feather Stitch Straight Center

1. Draw or follow a line. Follow Step 1 of the feather stitch (at left), with **A** and **C** on the line.

2. Repeat Step 1, alternating the stitches from right to left. To end the stitch, go down at **D**.

Feather Stitch Single

1. Draw or follow a line. Follow Step 1 of the feather stitch (above), with **A** and **C** on the line.

2. Repeat Step 1 to finish the row. To end the stitch, go down at **D**.

Feather Stitch Piggyback

1. Follow Steps 1 and 2 of the feather stitch (above left).

2. In one motion, go down at **D**, parallel to **B** of the first stitch, and up at **E** below the second stitch. Loop the working thread under the tip of the needle. Pull the needle through the fabric.

3. Repeat Steps 1 and 2 to finish the row. To end the stitch, go down at **F**.

Feather Stitch Closed

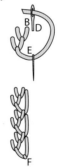

1. Draw or follow 2 parallel lines. *Follow Step 1 of the feather stitch (above left), with **A** on the left line and **B** and **C** on the right line.

2. Follow Step 2 of the feather stitch, with **D** close to **A** of the previous stitch and both **D** and **E** on the right line.

3. Repeat from *, alternating the stitches from right to left. To end the stitch, go down at **F**.

Maidenhair Fern Stitch

1. Follow Step 1 of the feather stitch (previous page). Work a second and third stitch slightly below and to the right.

2. Follow Step 2 of the feather stitch. Work a second and third stitch slightly below and to the left.

3. Repeat, alternating 3 close stitches to the right and to the left. To end the stitch, go down at **D**.

Maidenhair Fern Stitch Single

1. Follow Step 1 of the maidenhair fern stitch (at left).

2. Repeat Step 1 to finish the row, working the next stitch with **B** directly below **A** of the first stitch. To end the stitch, go down at **D**.

Feather and Chain Stitch

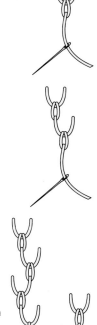

1. Follow Step 1 of the feather stitch (previous page). Work a chain stitch (page 120) inside the loop and below the feather stitch.

2. Repeat Step 1, working a feather stitch to the left and a chain stitch inside the loop ending below it.

3. Repeat Steps 1 and 2 to finish the row. To end the stitch, go down at **F**, which can be after a feather or a chain stitch.

Feather and Chain Stitch Variation

Follow the directions for the feather and chain stitch (above right) with the chain stitch angled to the right and to the left.

Feather and Chain Stitch Single

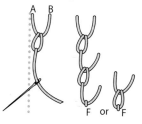

1. Follow Step 1 of the feather stitch single (previous page), working a chain stitch (page 120) below, inside the loop and on the line.

2. Repeat Step 1 to finish the row. To end the stitch, go down at **F**, which can be after a feather or a chain stitch.

Fly Stitches

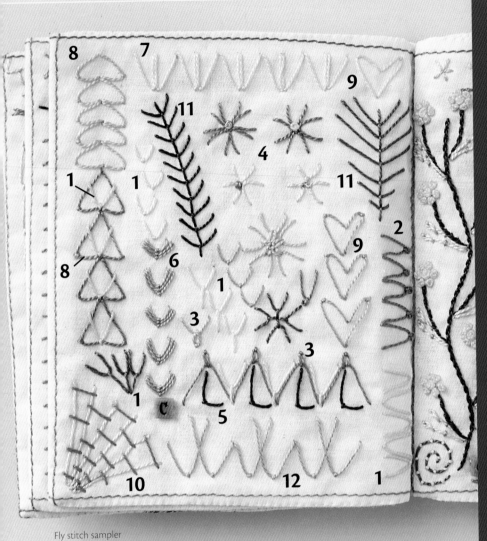

Fly stitch sampler

The fly stitch is suitable for twisted threads, silk embroidery ribbon, or floss. It can be stitched as a single unit to create a shape, or individual stitches can be grouped into a border row. The center and tips of the stitch can be embellished with individual or detail stitches.

Decorative Stitches

1. Fly Stitch (page 129)

2. Fly Stitch Knotted (page 129)

3. Fly and Loop Stitch (page 129)

4. Fly Stitch Flower (page 129)

5. Fly Stitch Offset (page 129)

6. Fly Stitch Stacked (page 129)

7. Fly Stitch Side by Side (page 130)

8. Triangle Stitch (page 130)

9. Heart Stitch (page 130)

10. Frilly Spider Web (page 130)

Border Row Stitches

11. Fern Stitch Modern (page 130)

12. Fly Stitch Crossed (page 130)

Fly Stitch

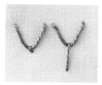

1. Come up at **A**. In one motion, go down at **B** and up at **C**. Loop the working thread under the tip of the needle. Pull the needle through the fabric.

2. To end the stitch, go down at **D** or a short distance away for a long tail.

Fly Stitch Knotted

1. Follow Step 1 of the fly stitch (at left).

2. Follow Step 2 for the French knot stitch (page 133), using the knot to catch the stitch.

Fly and Loop Stitch

1. Follow Step 1 of the fly stitch (at left). Work a lazy daisy stitch (page 135) inside the loop, catching the stitch.

2. To end the stitch, go down at **F**.

Fly Stitch Flower

1. Draw the lines for the petals with an erasable marker. The line represents the center of each stitch and is a guide only.

2. Choose from the fly stitch, fly stitch knotted, or fly and loop stitch (above). Work the stitches in the order shown.

Optional: Work a French knot stitch (page 133) in the center of the flower.

3-petal

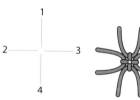

4-petal

5-petal

Fly Stitch Offset

1. Come up at **A**. In one motion, go down at **B** and up at **C**. Loop the working thread under the tip of the needle. Pull the needle through the fabric.

2. To end the stitch, go down at **D**.

Fly Stitch Stacked

1. Follow the directions for the fly stitch (above left).

2. Work a second and third stitch below the first.

Fly Stitch Side by Side

1. Follow Step 1 of the fly stitch (page 129).

2. Work a second stitch to the right. To end the stitch, go down at **D**.

Triangle Stitch

1. Follow the directions for the fly stitch offset (page 129), with **A** above **B** and with **C** to the left.

2. Work a second stitch angled to the right, stitching into points **A** and **B** of the first stitch.

Heart Stitch

1. Follow the directions for the fly stitch offset (page 129), with **A** above **B** and with **C** slightly above **A** and angled to the left.

2. Work a second stitch angled to the right, stitching into points **A** and **B** of the first stitch, with **C** slightly above **A**.

Frilly Spider Web

1. Follow the directions for the fly stitch (page 129), making an elongated stitch. Stitch 2 more stitches.

2. Work a straight stitch (page 132) across the top of each stitch; work a second and third row below.

3. Work a straight stitch below the first row, connecting adjacent sides of each fly stitch. Work a second row below.

Fern Stitch Modern

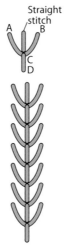

1. Work a straight stitch (page 132). Follow the directions for the fly stitch with a long tail (page 129), *with **A** and **B** even with the top of the straight stitch and **C** even with the bottom of the straight stitch.

2. To finish the row, repeat from *.

Fly Stitch Crossed

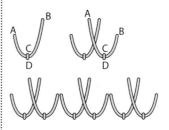

1. *Follow the directions for the fly stitch (page 129), with **B** higher than **A**.

2. Work a second stitch, with **A** higher than **B** and crossed over the previous stitch. To finish the row, repeat from *.

Knotted and Straight Stitches

These stitches are suitable for twisted threads, silk embroidery ribbon, or floss.

The border row stitches can also be used to create a shape; the individual stitches can be grouped into a border row.

Knotted and straight stitch sampler

Border Row Stitches

1. Coral Stitch (page 132)

2. Backstitch (page 132)

3. Outline Stitch (page 132)

4. Couched Stitch (page 132)

Decorative Stitches

5. Lacy Web Stitch (page 132)

6. Straight Stitch (page 132)

7. Straight Stitch Flower (page 133)

8. Stamen Stitch (page 133)

9. Pistil Stitch (page 133)

10. French Knot Stitch (page 133)

11. French Knot Stitch Flower (page 133)

12. Knobby Cobbleweb Stitch (page 133)

Coral Stitch

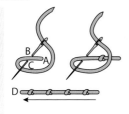

1. Draw or follow a line. Come up at **A** and hold the working thread on the line. *In one motion, go down at **B** and up at **C** slightly angled to the left. Loop the working thread under the tip of the needle.

2. Pull the needle through the fabric. To finish the row, repeat from *. To finish the stitch, go down at **D** a slight distance from the last knot.

Backstitch

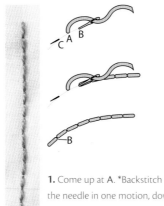

1. Come up at **A**. *Backstitch the needle in one motion, down at **B** and up at **C**. Pull the needle through the fabric.

2. **C** now becomes **A**. To finish the row, repeat from *. To end the stitch, go down at **B**.

Outline Stitch

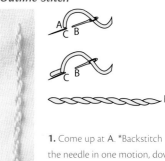

1. Come up at **A**. *Backstitch the needle in one motion, down at **B** and up at **C**. Pull the needle through the fabric.

2. Repeat from * to the end of the row, with **C** of the next stitch next to **B** of the previous stitch. To finish the stitch, go down at **B**.

Couched Stitch

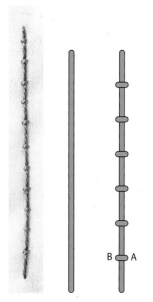

Stitch a length of thread onto the fabric; knot and cut the end. *Come up though the fabric with a second thread at **A**. Go down at **B**, stitching over the first thread. To finish the row, repeat from *.

Lacy Web Stitch

1. Draw the lines with an erasable marker. Stitch each line with a backstitch (above).

2. *Work a row of fly stitches (page 129) connecting across the top edge of the web. Work a second row below, into the first row.

3. To finish, repeat from *, working as many rows as needed.

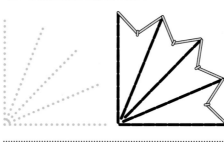

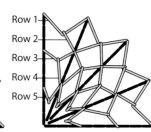

Row 1
Row 2
Row 3
Row 4
Row 5

Straight Stitch

Come up at **A** and go down at **B** a short distance from **A**.

Straight Stitch Flower

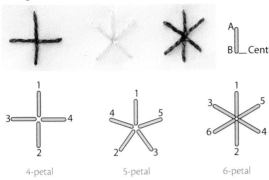

4-petal 5-petal 6-petal

Draw the lines for the petals with an erasable marker. Work the straight stitches (previous page) in the order shown.

Optional: Work a French knot (below) in the center of the flower.

note

The pistil stitch (below) or stamen stitch (at right) could also be used for the petals.

Stamen Stitch

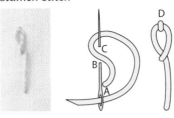

1. Come up at **A**. In one motion, go down at **B** and up at **C**, looping the working thread under the tip of the needle.

2. Pull the needle through the fabric. To finish the stitch, go down at **D**.

Pistil Stitch

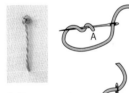

1. Come up at **A**. Holding the needle a short distance away and close to the fabric, wrap the thread 1–3 times over the needle.

2. Go down at **B**. Pull the needle and thread through the wrapped stitches and the fabric.

French Knot Stitch

1. Come up at **A**. Holding the needle close to the fabric, wrap the thread around the needle 1–5 times.

2. Pull the thread tight. Hold the end of the tail of thread with your thumb. Go down at **B**. Pull the needle and thread through the fabric.

French Knot Stitch Flower

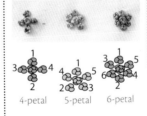

4-petal 5-petal 6-petal

1. Work a 3-wrap French knot stitch (at left) for the center.

2. With the same thread or a different color, work four to six 2-wrap French knots around the center in the order shown, stitching close to the center or farther away.

Knobby Cobbleweb Stitch

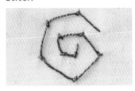

Draw a circle with an erasable marker. Beginning at the outer edge, stitch the coral stitch (previous page) around the edge, spiraling to the center.

Lazy Daisy Stitches

Lazy daisy stitch sampler

The lazy daisy stitch is suitable for twisted threads, silk embroidery ribbon, or floss. It can be stitched as a single unit to create a shape, or the individual stitches can be grouped into a border row. The bottom and tip of the stitch can be embellished with individual or detail stitches.

Decorative Stitches

Lazy Daisy Stitch

1. Come up at **A**. In one motion, go down at **B** and up at **C**. Loop the working thread under the tip of the needle. Pull the needle through the fabric.

2. To end the stitch, go down at **D** or a short distance away for a longer stitch.

Lazy Daisy Bullion Tip Stitch

1. Come up at **A**. In one motion, go down at **B** and up at **C**. Wrap the thread around the needle 2 or 3 times.

2. Pull the needle through the fabric. To finish the stitch, go down at **D** just beyond the wraps.

Lazy Daisy Knot Tip Stitch

1. Follow Step 1 of the lazy daisy stitch (at left).

2. Holding the needle close to the fabric, wrap the thread 1–3 times over the needle. Go down at **D**. Pull the needle and thread through the wrapped stitches and the fabric.

Lazy Daisy Stitch Flower

1. Draw the lines for the petals with an erasable marker. Work the stitches in the order shown.

2. Choose from the lazy daisy stitch, lazy daisy bullion tip stitch, or lazy daisy knot tip stitch (above).

Optional: Work a French knot stitch (page 133) in the center of the flower.

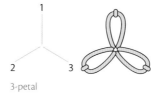

3-petal

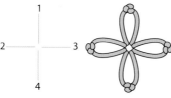

4-petal

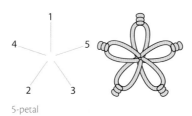

5-petal

Lazy Daisy Piggyback Stitch

Follow Step 1 of the lazy daisy stitch (above left). Work a smaller stitch inside the first stitch. To finish the stitch, go down at **D**.

Russian Chain Stitch

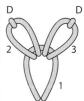

Follow Step 1 of the lazy daisy stitch (above left). Work 2 smaller stitches inside the first stitch as shown.

Lazy Daisy Plaited Stitch

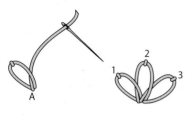

1. Follow the directions for the lazy daisy stitch (page 135). *Come up at **A**, and place the needle under the right half of the previous stitch.

2. Work a second lazy daisy stitch. Repeat from * to work a third stitch.

Optional: More petals can be stitched to complete a flower.

Berry Stitch

Follow the directions for the lazy daisy stitch (page 135). Work a longer second stitch around the first.

Looped Tendril Stitch

1. Follow Step 1 of the lazy daisy stitch (page 135). *In one motion, go down at **B** (outside, to the right of, and longer than the previous stitch) and up at **C**.

2. Repeat from *, stitching a third loop longer and to the right of the previous loop.

3. To end the stitch, go down at **D**.

Bumble Bee Stitch

1. Draw the lines for the body and wings with an erasable marker.

2. Follow the directions for the berry stitch (above center), working the body first and then the wings as numbered.

3. Work 2 straight stitches (page 132) each for antennae and legs, if desired.

Butterfly Stitch

1. Follow the directions for the lazy daisy bullion tip stitch (page 135).

2. Follow the directions for the looped tendril stitch (above right), working a separate stitch for each wing.

3. Work 2 straight stitches (page 132) each for the antennae and the legs.

Dragonfly Stitch

1. Draw the lines for the body and wings with an erasable marker.

2. Follow the directions for the lazy daisy stitch (page 135). Work 3 straight stitches (page 132) down the body as shown.

3. Follow the directions for the lazy daisy stitch (page 135) for each wing. Stitch 2 French knot stitches (page 133) for the eyes.

Wrapped, Whipped, and Covered Stitches

These stitches are suitable for twisted threads or floss. They can be stitched as a single unit to create a shape, or the individual stitches can be grouped into a border row. The tips of the stitch can be embellished with individual or detail stitches.

Wrapped, whipped, and covered stitch sampler

Decorative Stitches

1. Bullion Stitch (page 138)

2. Bullion Stitch Loop (page 138)

3. Bullion Stitch Rose (page 138)

4. Bullion Stitch Daisy (page 138)

5. Whip-Stitch Star (page 138)

6. Jill's Flower Stitch (page 138)

7. Jess's Flower Stitch (page 139)

8. Tiny Dragonfly Stitch (page 139)

9. Barnacle Stitch (page 139)

10. Gwen's Rose Stitch (page 139)

11. Frilled Petal Stitch (page 139)

12. Frilled Leaf Stitch (page 139)

Bullion Stitch

1. Come up at **A**. In one motion, go down at **B** and up at **C**, but do not pull the needle through the fabric.

2. Measure the distance between **A** and **B**; wrap the thread clockwise over the needle to equal the distance. Hold onto the needle and wraps as you gently pull the needle away from you and through the fabric and wraps.

3. Pull the wraps back toward you, keeping the wraps even. To end the stitch, go down at **D**.

Bullion Stitch Loop

1. Follow Step 1 for the bullion stitch (at left), with points **A** and **B** close together.

2. Wrap the thread 15 or more times. Follow the remaining directions.

Bullion Stitch Rose

1. Draw the lines for the petals with an erasable marker. Work three 3-wrap French knot stitches (page 133) into the center.

2. Follow the directions of the bullion stitch (at left). Work the stitches in the order shown.

Bullion Stitch Daisy

1. Draw the lines for the petals with an erasable marker.

2. Follow the directions of the bullion stitch loop (above center). Work the stitches in the order shown.

Optional: Work a French knot stitch (page 133) in the center of the flower.

Whip-Stitch Star

1. Stitch 3 straight stitches (page 132); stitch a short stitch across the center of the stitches.

2. Come up at **A**. Go under spokes 6 and 2. *Whip the thread over spoke 2 and then under spokes 2 and 4. Pull the thread close to the center.

3. Repeat, *whipping the thread over a spoke, then under the same spoke and the next spoke. To end the stitch, go down at **B** after the last spoke is covered.

Jill's Flower Stitch

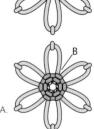

1. Follow the directions of the lazy daisy stitch flower (page 135) with 5 or 6 petals. Come up at **A**.

2. Follow the directions for the whip-stitch star (at left) from *, treating each lazy daisy stitch as a spoke. Work 3 rows around the center. To end the stitch, go down at **B**.

Jess's Flower Stitch

1. Follow the directions for the fly stitch flower (page 129) with 4 petals. Come up at **A**.

2. Follow the directions for the whip-stitch star (previous page) from *, working each spoke. To end the stitch, go down at **B**.

Optional: Work a French knot stitch (page 133) in the center of the flower.

Tiny Dragonfly Stitch

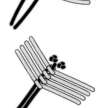

1. Follow the directions for the lazy daisy stitch (page 135). *Come up at **A**. Go under the lazy daisy stitch; then whip the thread over and then under again. Go down at **B**.

2. Repeat from * to stitch 3 more wings. Stitch 2 French knot stitches (page 133) for the eyes.

Barnacle Stitch

1. Draw 3 lines with an erasable marker; stitch with straight stitches (page 132).

2. Buttonhole Stitch: Come up at **A**. *Go under the base stitch; loop the working thread under the tip of the needle. Pull the thread firmly around the base stitch. The buttonhole stitch is worked off of the embroidered stitch and does not go through the fabric.

3. Repeat from * to finish the stitching the base. To finish the stitch, go down at **B**.

Gwen's Rose Stitch

1. Draw a circle with an erasable marker; stitch 6 chain stitches (page 120) around the circle. **Follow the directions for the buttonhole stitch (Barnacle Stitch, Step 2, above right). The buttonhole stitch is worked off of the embroidered stitch and does not go through the fabric.

2. Work the stitches around the outer edge of each chain stitch. To finish the stitch, go down at **B**. Repeat from **, working the stitches around the inner edge of each chain stitch.

3. Fill in the center with 3-wrap French knot stitches (page 133).

Frilled Petal Stitch

1. Stitch a fly stitch (page 129). Follow the directions for the buttonhole stitch (Barnacle Stitch, Step 2, above right). The buttonhole stitch is worked off of the embroidered stitch and does not go through the fabric.

2. Repeat from * (of the buttonhole stitch), working around half of the loop. To finish the stitch, go down at **B**.

Frilled Leaf Stitch

1. Stitch a lazy daisy stitch (page 135). Follow the directions for the buttonhole stitch (Barnacle Stitch, Step 2, above). The buttonhole stitch is worked off of the embroidered stitch and does not go through the fabric.

2. Repeat from * (of the buttonhole stitch), working around half of the loop. To finish the stitch, go down at **B**.

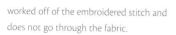

Silk Ribbon Embroidery Stitches

The decorative stitches are suitable for silk embroidery ribbon. The ribbon-work stitches are suitable for silk embroidery ribbon or woven ribbon. The individual stitches can be stitched as a single unit or to create a shape.

Silk ribbon embroidery stitch sampler

Decorative Stitches

1. Ribbon Stitch (page 141)

2. Ribbon Loop Stitch (page 141)

3. Pointed Petal Stitch (page 141)

4. Silk Ribbon Flower Stitch (page 141)

5. Mum Stitch (page 141)

6. Whipped Stitch (page 142)

7. Whipped Posy Stitch (page 142)

8. Whipped Rose Stitch (page 142)

9. Woven Rose Stitch (page 142)

10. Pin Rose Stitch (page 142)

11. Accordion Rose Stitch (page 142)

12. Elegant Butterfly Stitch (page 142)

Ribbon Stitch

1. Come up at **A**. Hold the ribbon flat against the fabric. Go down at **B** through the ribbon.

2. Form a curved tip by gently pulling the ribbon through the stitch.

Ribbon Loop Stitch

 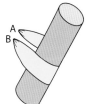

Come up at **A** and down at **B**. Insert a porcupine quill or straw into the center of the loop; pull the ribbon through the fabric to the desired length.

Pointed Petal Stitch

1. Come up at **A** and down at **B**. Pull the ribbon through the fabric to form a point at the tip. Set this needle aside.

2. Thread a needle with sewing thread or floss. Come up at **C** through the ribbon; go down at **D** at the tip of the ribbon. Knot and cut both the thread and ribbon.

Silk Ribbon Flower Stitch

1. Draw the lines for the petals with an erasable marker. Work the stitches in the order shown.

 note

For the ribbon loop stitch, draw the lines very short, as shown.

2. Choose from the ribbon stitch, ribbon loop stitch, or pointed petal stitch (above).

Optional: Work a French knot stitch (page 133) in the center of the flower.

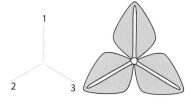

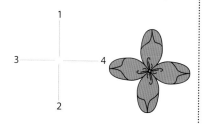

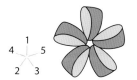

Mum Stitch

1. Draw a large circle, a medium circle, and a small circle with an erasable marker. Beginning on the medium circle, *stitch a ribbon stitch (above left), ending on the outer circle. Repeat from * to finish the circle.

2. Beginning on the small circle, **stitch a ribbon stitch between each of the previous stitches. Repeat from ** to finish the circle.

3. Fill the center with French knot stitches (page 133).

Optional: Stitch straight stitches (page 132) in between each petal from Step 2.

Whipped Stitch

1. Come up at **A** and down at **B** to stitch a straight stitch. Keep the ribbon flat. Come up at **A**.

2. Whip the needle under and around the stitch 3 times to the right. Reverse direction and whip the needle under and around the stitch 2 times to the left. Go down at **C**.

Whipped Posy Stitch

1. Draw the lines for the petals with an erasable marker. Work straight stitches in the order shown.

2. Follow the directions from Step 2 of the whipped stitch (at left) for each straight stitch. Work a 3–5-wrap French knot stitch (page 133) in the center of the flower.

Whipped Rose Stitch

1. Draw the lines for the petals with an erasable marker. Work straight stitches in the order shown.

2. Follow the directions from Step 2 of the whipped stitch (at left) for each straight stitch. Fill the center with 3-wrap French knot stitches (page 133).

Woven Rose Stitch

 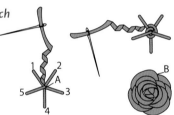

1. Draw the lines for the petals with an erasable marker. Thread a needle with perle cotton and work straight stitches (page 132) in the order shown. Knot and cut the thread.

2. With silk embroidery ribbon, come up at **A**, twisting the ribbon slightly clockwise.

3. Working counterclockwise around the base, thread the needle over and under the spokes, pulling the ribbon through each spoke. To end the stitch, go down through the fabric at **B**.

Pin Rose Stitch

1. Follow Step 1 of the lazy daisy stitch (page 135), looping the working thread under the base of the stitch. Loop the thread a second and third time around the needle.

2. Place your thumb on the thread wraps and needle; pull the needle through the fabric. Go down at **D**. To end the stitch, come up at **E** and down at **F**.

Accordion Rose Stitch

Come up at **A**. Measure 2" of ribbon; from that measurement, stitch down the middle of the length of the ribbon to the beginning end. Go down at **A**. Pull the needle through the ribbon to form the petals.

Elegant Butterfly Stitch

1. Draw the lines for the wings with an erasable marker. With silk ribbon, stitch 4 ribbon loop stitches. Stitch a straight stitch (page 132) for the body.

2. With perle cotton or floss, stitch 2 pistil stitches (page 133) for the antennae and legs.

Bead Embroidery Stitches

These stitches are suitable for all sizes and shapes of seed beads.

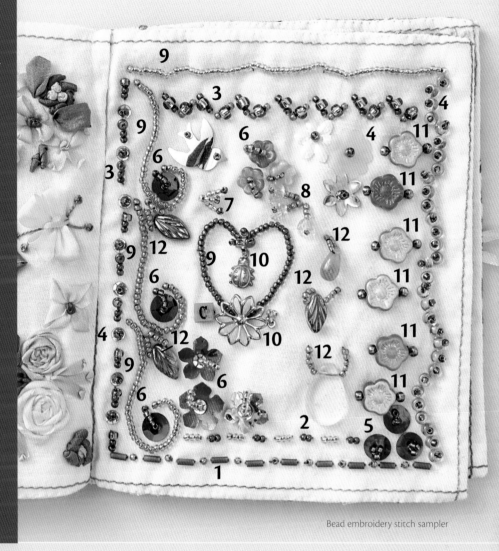

Bead embroidery stitch sampler

Decorative Stitches

1. Single Bead Stitch (page 144)

2. Grouped Bead Stitch (page 144)

3. Bead Combination Stitch (page 144)

4. Stacked Bead Stitch (page 144)

5. Picot Tip Stitch (page 144)

6. Bead Cascade Stitch (page 144)

7. Beaded Stamen Stitch (page 145)

8. Stem and Flower Stitch (page 145)

9. Continuous Bead Stitch (page 145)

10. Beaded Charms (page 145)

11. Top-to-Bottom Hole Charms (page 145)

12. Side-to-Side Hole Charms (page 145)

Single Bead Stitch

1. Come up and thread a bead onto the needle, placing the bead flat against the fabric. Go down beyond the edge of the bead.

2. Come up and thread the needle through the bead a second time, again going down beyond the edge of the bead in the same hole as before. Knot the thread after every 4 stitches.

Grouped Bead Stitch

Follow the directions of the single bead stitch (at left), but with 2 or 3 of the same size and type of bead. Knot the thread after every 2 stitches.

Bead Combination Stitch

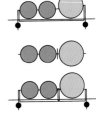

1. Follow the directions of the single bead stitch (at left), but with a group of different sizes or shapes of beads.

2. Come up at **A**, between the large and small beads, and go down at **B** to couch the bead thread. Knot the thread after every 2 stitches.

Stacked Bead Stitch

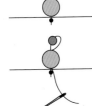

1. Base Bead: Come up through a large bead.

2. Stopper Bead: Thread a smaller bead onto the needle. Then thread the needle back through the base bead and down. Knot the thread.

Picot Tip Stitch

1. Base Bead: Come up through a large bead.

2. Picot Tip: Thread 3 smaller beads onto the needle; thread the needle back through the base bead and down. Knot the thread after every stitch.

Bead Cascade Stitch

1. Base Bead: Come up through a large bead.

2. Cascade: Thread 3 or more smaller beads onto the needle; go down just beyond the edge of the large bead. Knot the thread after every stitch.

Beaded Stamen Stitch

1. Come up and thread 4 or more smaller beads onto the needle.

2. Holding onto the last bead, thread the needle back through the remaining beads and down. Knot the thread after every stitch.

Stem and Flower Stitch

1. Come up and thread 3 smaller beads, a flower bead, and a smaller bead onto the needle.

2. Holding onto the last bead, thread the needle back through the remaining beads and down. Knot the thread after every stitch.

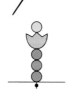

Continuous Bead Stitch

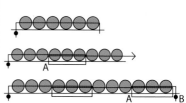

1. Come up and *thread 6 beads onto the needle, laying the row of beads flat against the fabric. Go down just beyond the edge of the last bead.

2. Come up at **A**, between the third and fourth bead in the row. Thread the needle through the remaining 3 beads in the row. To finish the row, continue from *.

3. To end the row, come up at **A**, go through the last 3 beads in the row, and go down at **B**. Knot the thread.

Beaded Charms

1. Come up through the hole in the charm and follow the directions for the stopper bead (Stacked Bead Stitch, Step 2, previous page).

2. Or come up through the hole in the charm and follow the directions for the cascade (Bead Cascade Stitch, Step 2, previous page).

Top-to-Bottom Hole Charms

Follow the directions for the bead combination stitch (previous page), with the charm in the middle of the group; couch on either side of the charm. Knot the thread after every stitch.

Side-to-Side Hole Charms

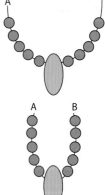

1. Come up at **A**; thread 5 smaller beads, a charm, and another 5 smaller beads onto the needle.

2. Go down at **B**. Knot the thread after every stitch.

Embroidered Buttons

Buttons can be stitched in place with twisted threads, floss, silk embroidery ribbon, or seed beads.

General Directions: To work embroidery stitches through the holes of the button, you will need to review Variations in Stitch Technique (page 39).

Ribbonwork flowers and trimmed trims sampler

Decorative Stitches

1. Stitched Buttons (page 147)

2. Stitched Buttons Fancy (page 147)

3. Embroidered Buttons: Lazy Daisy Stitch (page 147)

4. Embroidered Buttons: French Knot Stitch (page 147)

5. Embroidered Buttons: Fly Stitch (page 147)

6. Embroidered Buttons: Blanket Stitch (page 147)

7. Embroidered Buttons: Chain Stitch (page 147)

8. Stacked Buttons (page 147)

9. Clustered Buttons (page 147)

10. Button Spider (page 147)

11. Button Flower (page 147)

12. Beaded Buttons (page 147)

Stitched Buttons

The holes of the button can be stitched in a variety of patterns.

Stitched Buttons Fancy

The holes of the button can be stitched in a variety of patterns, with the stitches extending beyond the edge of the button.

Embroidered Buttons: Lazy Daisy Stitch

Lazy daisy stitches (page 135) come out of the holes in the button.

Embroidered Buttons: French Knot Stitch

French knot stitches (page 133) are worked around the button's outer edge.

Embroidered Buttons: Fly Stitch

Fly stitches (page 129) are worked with the loop into the holes in the button.

Embroidered Buttons: Blanket Stitch

Blanket stitches (page 116) are worked into the holes in the button and are formed around the button's outer edge.

Embroidered Buttons: Chain Stitch

Chain stitches (page 120) are worked around the button's outer edge.

Stacked Buttons

A small button is stitched on top of a large button.

Clustered Buttons

Buttons are stitched clustered into a group.

Button Spider

Stitch 2 buttons—1 for the head and 1 for the body. Stitch the legs with the fly stitch offset (page 129); stitch the eyes with the French knot stitch (page 133).

Button Flower

Stitch a loop stitch leaves and stalk (page 121). Stitch a button at the top of the stalk.

Beaded Buttons

Follow the directions for any of the beaded stitches that require a base bead.

Ribbonwork Flowers and Trimmed Trims

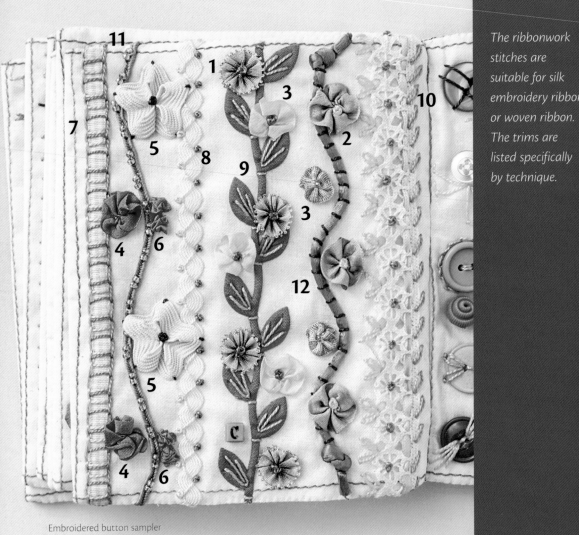

The ribbonwork stitches are suitable for silk embroidery ribbon or woven ribbon. The trims are listed specifically by technique.

Embroidered button sampler

Ribbonwork Techniques

1. Rosette (page 149)

2. Double Rosette (page 149)

3. Ribbon Posy (page 149)

4. Old Rose (page 150)

5. Rickrack Flower (page 150)

6. Detail Flower (page 150)

Trimmed Trims

7. Ribbon Trim (page 151)

8. Rickrack Trim (page 151)

9. Leaf Trim (page 151)

10. Lace Trim (page 151)

11. Soutache Trim (page 151)

12. Rayon Cord Trim (page 151)

General Ribbonwork Directions

1. Cut a length of ribbon using the ribbon measurement guide.

2. Thread a small sharp needle with thread.

3. Come up through the fabric.

4. Cut the thread after stitching each flower.

RIBBON MEASUREMENT GUIDE

Flower	Woven ribbon width				Silk embroidery ribbon		
	⅛″	4mm	¼″	7mm	⅜″	½″	13mm
Rosette	1″		2″		3″	4″	
Double rosette	2″		4″		6″	8″	
Ribbon posy	1″		2″		3″	4″	
Old rose	1½″		3″		4¼″	6″	

Rosette

 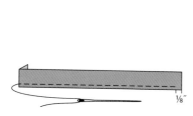 

1. Come up through the ribbon ⅛″ from the raw and bottom selvage edges.

2. Gather stitch along the bottom selvage edge, stopping ¼″ from the opposite raw edge; fold the edge under. The needle should be on the wrong side of the ribbon.

3. Go down through the ribbon and fabric close to the beginning stitch. Pull the thread to create the center of the flower. Knot the thread. Tackstitch the center and outer edges of the ribbon.

Double Rosette

1. Fold the length of ribbon in half. Come up through the ribbon ⅛″ from the raw and bottom selvage edges.

2. Follow Step 2 (note that the edge is already folded) and Step 3 of the rosette (above).

Ribbon Posy

1. Come up through the ribbon ⅛″ from the raw and top selvage edges.

2. Gather stitch at an angle down to the bottom selvage edge and continue along the bottom edge; stop and angle to the top selvage and raw edge.

3. Go down through the ribbon and fabric close to the beginning stitch. Pull the thread to create the center of the flower. Knot the thread. Tackstitch the center and outer edges of the ribbon.

Old Rose

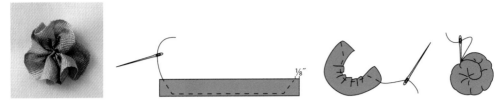

1. Come up through the ribbon ⅛″ from the raw and top selvage edges. Follow Step 2 of the ribbon posy (page 149).

2. Pull the thread to create the flower. Wrap the ribbon around the center; go down through the fabric at the edge of the rose.

Rickrack Flower

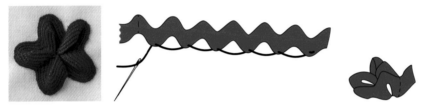

1. Knot the thread at a lower curve. Whipstitch through the next 5 lower curves.

2. Pull to gather and knot the thread. Cut off the excess rickrack. Stitch a seam joining the 2 end lower curves.

Detail Flower

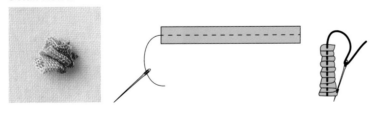

1. Cut 1″–2″ of 4 mm ribbon. Come up through the fabric and the center of the ribbon close to a raw edge. Gather stitch through the center, stopping just short of the raw edge.

2. Pull to gather and go down just beyond the beginning edge of the ribbon.

General Trim Directions

Stitch or glue the ribbon in place first.

Ribbon Trim

Embroidery suggestions are blanket stitch (page 116), chain stitch (page 120), chevron stitch (page 123), herringbone stitch (page 123), cross stitch row (page 124), feather stitch closed (page 126).

Rickrack Trim

Embroidery suggestions are bell flower stitch (page 118), fly stitch (page 129), French knot stitch (page 133), lazy daisy stitch (page 135), single bead stitch (page 144), stacked bead stitch (page 144).

Leaf Trim

Embroidery suggestions are fly stitch (page 129), straight stitch (page 132), French knot stitch (page 133), lazy daisy stitch (page 135), single bead stitch (page 144), grouped bead stitch (page 144).

Lace Trim

Embroidery suggestions are French knot stitch (page 133), lazy daisy stitch (page 135), single bead stitch (page 144), grouped bead stitch (page 144).

Option: A thin ribbon can also be inserted through any loops of a lace trim using a bodkin.

Soutache Trim

Embroidery suggestions are blanket stitch (page 116), couched stitch (page 132), lazy daisy stitch (page 135), single bead stitch (page 144), grouped bead stitch (page 144).

Rayon Cord Trim

Pin the cord in place or hold in place with your hand. Embroidery suggestions are blanket stitch (page 116), cross stitch (page 124), fly stitch (page 129), couched stitch (page 132), lazy daisy stitch (page 135), bullion stitch (page 138), bead cascade stitch (page 144).

THE BASICS

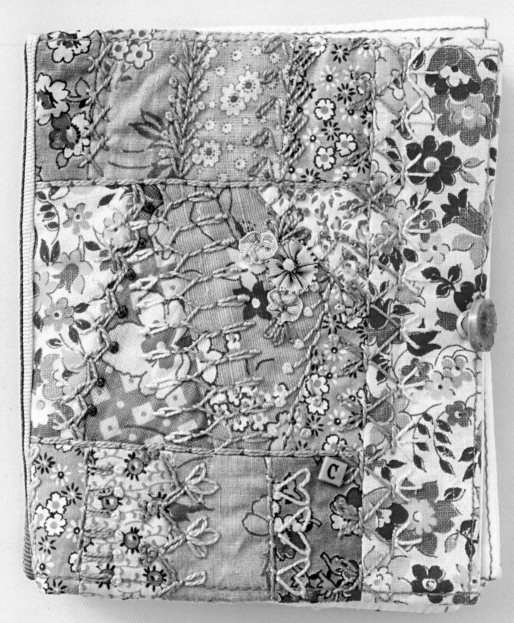

Embroidery Journal (page 43)

Sewing Basics

HAND SEWING TOOLS

These are the basic supplies and essentials that I keep on hand once the base is pieced and ribbon, trims, and lace are to be attached.

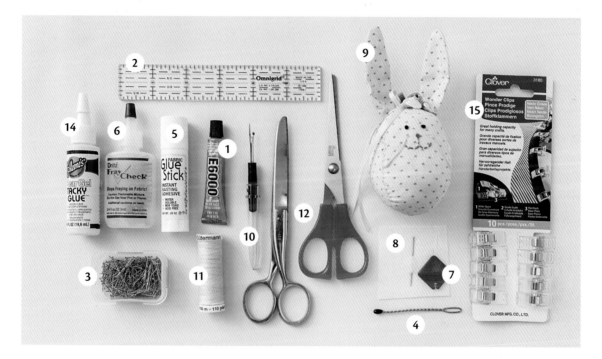

1. E6000 Craft Adhesive to attach metal or glass items

2. 6" clear quilter's ruler with ⅛" and ¼" markings

3. Appliqué pins for trims or appliqués

4. Bodkin to thread ribbon through eyelet lace

5. Fabric glue stick

6. Fray Check, used on fabric, lace, and ribbon to keep the edges from fraying

7. Needle threader

8. Needles, small sharps

9. Pincushion

10. Seam ripper

11. Sewing thread to match the project

12. Scissors, fabric and craft

13. Sulky KK 2000 Temporary Spray Adhesive (not shown)

14. Tacky glue, to attach small fiber items

15. Wonder Clips by Clover to hold binding in place

HAND SEWING SPECIFICS

- Prewash all fabrics before you begin piecing or stitching. If the finished project ever needs to be washed, the fabric will not shrink.

- When working with any stabilizer or backing product, be sure to follow the manufacturer's recommended instructions.

- Gently clean any vintage laces or trims using a mild hand soap and water; dry flat on a towel and lightly press if needed.

Embroidery Basics

EMBROIDERY TOOLS

These are the basic supplies and essentials that I keep on hand for embroidery and embellishment.

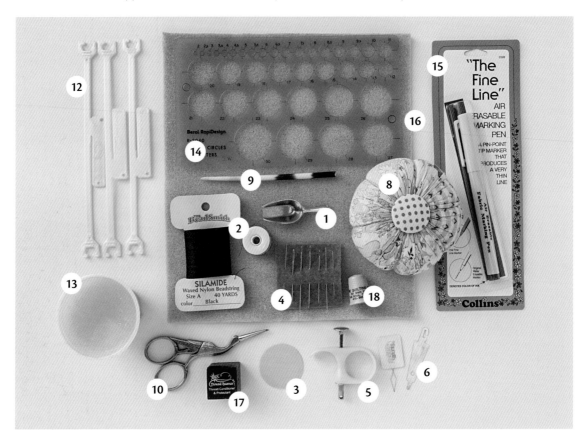

1. Bead scoop for picking up loose beads

2. Beading thread: Nymo and Silamide

3. Needle grabber to pull the needle through layers of fabric

4. Needles: beading, chenille, cotton darner, crewel, embroidery, milliners, sharps

5. Needle Puller

6. Needle threaders

7. Full-spectrum light (not shown)

8. Pincushion

9. Porcupine quill or cocktail straw for use in silk ribbon embroidery

10. Scissors: embroidery

11. Segmented bead dish (not shown)

12. Stitch Bow organizers to keep floss from tangling

13. Synthetic beeswax to condition beading thread

14. Circle templates

15. The Fine Line Air Erasable Marking Pen to establish a line or starting point for an embroidery design

16. Thermal bead mat to keep beads from sliding around

17. Thread Heaven conditioner to minimize knotting of embroidery and sewing threads

18. Thimble

EMBROIDERY STITCHING AIDS

Embroidery templates

Even the most experienced embroider knows that stitching a row or shape evenly can be made easier with a few drawn lines. I have developed these embroidery templates for that basic purpose. There are four templates offering a variety of lines, shapes, images, and rulers.

I suggest that you use a fine-line air-erasable marker to draw the lines. I also suggest that you test the marker first on a scrap piece of your fabric to make sure that the line will, in fact, erase. Most lightly drawn lines will disappear within a few hours; a heavily drawn line may take a few days to erase.

Blanket and buttonhole stitch sampler: the templates were used for the outline of the half-heart, zigzag, and curved lines

Chain and looped stitch sampler: the templates were used for the outline of the heart and the curved vine.

Feather stitch sampler: the templates were used for the outline of the heart and the curved vine.

Marked Ruler Tapes

When stitching a border row, I also find it helpful to use marked fabric tape as a guideline to create evenly spaced stitches. There are a few premarked tapes available for purchase, or you can make your own by marking a tape, such as the Quilter's ¼ Inch Ruler Tape, with the guidelines offered on the templates.

EMBROIDERY SPECIFICS

- When working with variegated, ombré, and space-dyed threads and ribbons, work with the colors as they come, rather than searching for a match or blend.

- To eliminate knots and tangles when using twisted threads, thread the needle with the twist running down the thread.

- Cut off a length of floss from the skein and split the threads in the amount you want to work with. Separate each thread individually from the group; then reassemble them to eliminate tangling.

- Use a pair of craft scissors to cut the metallic threads, trims, or lace, as the metallic finish can dull your good embroidery scissors.

- When embroidering with silk embroidery ribbons, the ribbon should lie flat against the fabric; however, the ribbon can twist once it is pulled through the fabric. If the ribbon is concave, hold the ribbon next to the fabric and then stitch. If the ribbon is convex, rub the ribbon until it is flat or concave.

- Nymo and Silamide beading threads are used double, with a knot in the tail. Synthetic beeswax will hold the thread together.

- When beading, knot the thread on the wrong side of the fabric as directed, then resume stitching.

Choosing the Correct Needle

The purpose of the needle is to make a hole in the fabric big enough for the thread or ribbon to pass through the fabric, but not so big that it will damage the fabric. As a general rule, the shaft of the needle should be the same thickness as the thread or ribbon. Needles are sized from low to high; the lower number, the larger needle.

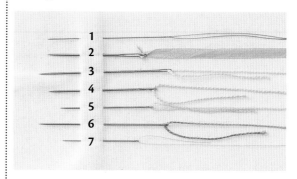

1. Beading: a thin, short, or long needle with a small eye, used for all types of beading threads

2. Chenille: a medium-length needle with a long eye that is suitable for silk embroidery ribbon

3. Cotton darner: a long needle with an oval eye that is used for twisted threads

4. Crewel (also called embroidery needles): a long needle with a long to medium eye that is wider than the shaft; used for twisted threads

5. Embroidery: a fine, thin needle with a long eye that is used for stranded floss

6. Milliners: a long needle with a shaft the same width the length of the needle and with a rounded small eye; used for twisted threads

7. Sharps: a shorter, fine needle with a small eye used for sewing thread

PROPER CUT LENGTHS AND KNOTS

- Cut the embroidery threads and flosses 16"–18" long.

- Cut the silk embroidery ribbons 12"–15" long.

- Cut metallic threads 14"–16" long.

- Cut the beading threads 1½ yards long; use double.

I knot my thread after it is cut and threaded through the needle. In most cases, I work with a stabilizer and lining, so the knot will never show. When working with silk embroidery ribbon, it is easier to hand stitch the beginning and the ending tail to the wrong side of the base with sewing thread.

Tips: Essential to the Eclectic

- Use Sulky KK 2000 Temporary Spray Adhesive to keep fabric in place while pinning and stitching.

- Use a glue stick to temporarily keep lace, ribbons, and trims in place while stitching.

- Serge or zigzag the outer raw edges of the fabric base to prevent fraying while you work the stitches.

- Use Fray Check to help keep lace, ribbons, and trims from fraying.

- Use Wonder Clips to hold binding or trim in place.

- Always wash your hands before working with the fabric base, embroidery threads, and ribbons.

- All of the threads and ribbons will naturally twist; if you periodically hold the fabric base upside down and let the thread and needle dangle down, the thread will unwind.

- Run the length of twisted thread or floss over Thread Heaven to prevent the tail of the thread from knotting or wrapping around the working portion of the thread.

- Buttonhole twist, rayon threads, and silk embroidery ribbon have a tendency to retain the fold from the packaging. Slightly moisten the length that you are working with and gently pass the thread or ribbon over the upright plate of a warm iron.

- Most hand-dyed threads and silk embroidery ribbons are colorfast; however, testing a sample by hand washing is always a good idea.

- Trims, appliqués, and buttons can be stitched to cover raw edges that are not caught in a seam.

- Take notes while you are embroidering, such as the number of wraps for the French knots or the number of strands of floss for a stitch.

- Think of a mistake as a design opportunity that you had not thought of yet. Once you repeat a mistake, it becomes another element in the design.

RESOURCES

I encourage you to shop at your favorite local or online small business. The store owners and their employees know what they have in stock, how to use their products, and where to get special items.

I would like to extend my special thanks and gratitude to the wonderful vendors who so generously provided the supplies that I used for the samples and projects included in this book.

FABRICS

Hoffman California Fabrics • Batik fabric • hoffmanfabrics.com

Moda Fabrics • Cotton fabric • modafabrics.com

Thai Silks • Silk fabric • thaisilks.com

EMBROIDERY THREADS AND RIBBONS

The Caron Collection • Hand-dyed perle cotton, cotton, silk floss • caron-net.com

Kreinik • Metallic thread, silk floss • kreinik.com

House of Textile Arts • Hand-dyed threads, cords, cocoons • textile-arts-international.com

Presencia America • Perle cotton, cotton floss • presenciaamerica.com

Rainbow Gallery • Silk and specialty silk perle and cotton threads • rainbowgallery.com

Thread Art • Silk embroidery ribbon • threadart.com

Valdani Inc. • Hand-dyed perle cotton and floss • valdani.com

NEEDLES

Colonial Needle Company • colonialneedle.com

John James Needles • jjneedles.com

PRODUCTS AND BOOKS

C&T Publishing • Timtex, fast2fuse, and other wonderful products • ctpub.com

Joggles • Felt houses, thread, other products • joggles.com

The Store on the Corner • Vintage and new ribbons and buttons, cotton and silk threads, and more christenbrown.com

 tip

■ If you see something you like while shopping, I suggest that you buy it. Otherwise, while working on a design inspiration four years later at midnight, you will be asking yourself, "Why didn't I buy that?"

■ Quantities: odd, even, how much should I buy? When designing a small wallhanging, these are the rules that I follow: If it is a large component, such as a doily or appliqué that could be used as a center design, then one should be enough. If it is a medium component, such as a 1″ button, then 4–5. If it is a smaller component, such as charms, buttons, or other items, then 10–15.